M000285165

TESTIMONIALS

There are two important reasons for you to read *Altruistic Business* by Gavin Watson. First, he actually organized his family business around altruistic principles, causing it to thrive. Second, he has read widely and lucidly explains the rationale for why altruism is an enlightened business strategy. Very few authors have combined theory and practice so well.

David Sloan Wilson
President, Prosocial World
Author of *This View of Life: Completing the Darwinian Revolution*

Gavin Watson is an inspirational business leader who transformed the Watson company from a traditional business model to one of radical empowerment and success. His writing challenged me to think about culture of empowerment way beyond my comfort level—as a vehicle of employee happiness and business success. The book chronicles the evolutionary necessity that underpins movements, like conscious capitalism and B-Corps, and explains why these frameworks are helping companies to evolve to be both purposeful and to win in the marketplace. This book is to be read, thought about, implemented, and shared. Enjoy.

David Reitz
President Gestalt Management
Former CEO Inventec Performance Chemicals USA LLC

Gavin Watson took over his family company, and set about boldly putting people at the core of his lean and agile business rejuvenation. By giving his loyal workers agency, autonomy and empowerment, he was able to harness their collective intelligence and group altruism to power his business to even greater success. Today, Gavin is at the forefront of a new breed of conscious capitalists applying Prosocial principles to overturn conventional business paradigms. This amazing book encapsulates his journey and is a must-read for every business CEO.

Dr. Exmond E DeCruz
CEO, Peakintelli Group

Gavin Watson was such a motivating leader, Trusted and believed in everyone who had the desire to work. My experience working with Gavin was phenomenal. He saw potential in me and gave me the opportunity to grow within his company. I would not hesitate to work for such a great leader like Gavin Watson.

Elida Rivera
Team Member, Watson Inc.

"Buisness as Usual" has some fatal flaws and has helped create a long list of social and environmnetal challanges that the global community has to address. Most business publications are theory heavy do little to shift our "win at all costs" predatory approach to business.

This book will change that. Based on Gavins lived experience and underpinned with solid science, its an easy read that will shift your business practice to a more human centric and fun place to work.

Glen McDermott
Founder, Red Rock Branding

Gavin has taken the time to integrate many fields of knowledge into a comprehensive yet understandable world view on the way human beings are wired and designed to work best. I have steadily been applying his precepts for building and leading small groups, and I find that they create very direct pathways to a simpler, happier, and more engaging workflow.

Elinor Slomba
Founder, Verge Arts Group

This is a great read for anyone who believes that as company leaders we can do better. Gavin helps the reader to lift up all base business assumptions and question their validity. He provides the opportunity to rethink the business model and to change it for the better based on solid principles and reasoning. Collaborative businesses outperform combative businesses. Buckets of business leadership wisdom provided in a practical manner.

Paul Murphy
Founder, Conscious Power Solutions

Altruistic Business

Altruistic Business

Why Conscious Businesses Outperform the Competition

Gavin Watson

PYP **Publish** Your Purpose

Copyright © 2023 Gavin Watson. All rights reserved.

No part of this publication shall be reproduced, transmitted, or sold in whole or in part in any form without prior written consent of the author, except as provided by the United States of America copyright law. Any unauthorized usage of the text without express written permission of the publisher is a violation of the author's copyright and is illegal and punishable by law. All trademarks and registered trademarks appearing in this guide are the property of their respective owners.

For permission requests, write to the publisher, addressed "Attention: Permissions Coordinator," at the address below.

Publish Your Purpose
141 Weston Street, #155
Hartford, CT, 06141

The opinions expressed by the Author are not necessarily those held by Publish Your Purpose.

Ordering Information: Quantity sales and special discounts are available on quantity purchases by corporations, associations, and others. For details, contact the publisher at orders@publishyourpurposepress.com.

Edited by: August Li, Jill Kramek, Tamera Bryant
Cover design by: Cornelia Murariu
Typeset by: Medlar Publishing Solutions Pvt Ltd., India

Printed in the United States of America.

ISBN: 978-1-955985-80-2 (hardcover)
ISBN: 978-1-955985-79-6 (paperback)
ISBN: 978-1-955985-81-9 (ebook)

Library of Congress Control Number: 2022912825

First edition, January 2023.

The information contained within this book is strictly for informational purposes. The material may include information, products, or services by third parties. As such, the Author and Publisher do not assume responsibility or liability for any third-party material or opinions. The publisher is not responsible for websites (or their content) that are not owned by the publisher. Readers are advised to do their own due diligence when it comes to making decisions.

Publish Your Purpose is a hybrid publisher of nonfiction books. Our authors are thought leaders, experts in their fields, and visionaries paving the way to social change—from food security to anti-racism. We give underrepresented voices power and a stage to share their stories, speak their truth, and impact their communities. Do you have a book idea you would like us to consider publishing? Please visit PublishYourPurpose.com for more information.

Dedication

For all my friends at Watson Inc., who ran multiple experiments and created an awesome place to work.

Acknowledgments

As you will see, these are predominantly not my ideas. Just like many who have come before me, I am standing on the shoulders of people who have dedicated their lives to philosophy and research. Here I have collected their hard work and organized it in a way that makes sense to me.

Evolutionary biologist David Sloan Wilson uses the analogy of an archipelago of disciplines. People devote their lives to research within their discipline but rarely look to connect the ideas that are emerging on their island with the ideas emerging on other islands.

As it happens, in my other "real life" I am a boatbuilder and a sailor. In my "business life," I have been sailing between these islands, gathering ideas, and seeing how they connect.

I saw many connections here and there and eventually I discovered the work of David Sloan Wilson. His expression of the theory of evolution brings together ideas from many islands and in the light of day binds them.

Table of Contents

PART 2

Introduction

WHAT IS THIS BOOK ABOUT?

Many businesses are run based on a misunderstanding, the idea that business is a competition, a survival of the fittest game. The fittest is supposed to be the most rational, value-calculating, and self-interested individual or company. As I will explain, this is objectively false. It may be subjectively true, but only to the extent that we persist in believing it.

Conscious business is based on evolutionary biology's current understanding of human evolution. For humans (and our businesses), it is not survival of the fittest individual, it is survival of the fittest group that counts. The fittest group is the most altruistic, compassionate, and generous individuals, company, or group of companies. As Charles Darwin (2019, 107) put it in *On the Origin of Species*, "Those communities, which included the greatest number of most sympathetic members, would flourish best and rear the greatest number of offspring."

Evolutionary biologists David Sloan Wilson and E.O Wilson (2007) phrased it this way, "Selfishness beats altruism within groups. Altruistic groups beat selfish groups. Everything else is commentary."

This book is about this change in perspective and why we can now say without hesitation that Conscious, Prosocial, Altruistic business is objectively true and shareholder Capitalism is objectively false. All that is needed is a system to prevent selfishness within a group. Fortunately we have this system thanks to the Nobel Prize-winning work of Elinor Ostrom and her collaboration with David Sloan Wilson (Wilson et al. 2010) in creating the Prosocial Core Design Principles.

EXPLAINING THE TITLE

What is altruism? It is an action taken for the benefit of others. The action may or may not be beneficial to the altruistic individual or group. There are many altruistic businesses just as there are many altruistic individuals. A conscious, altruistic business is one that recognizes that its performance depends on creating an altruistic group within the business (conscious culture) and an altruistic group economic ecosystem outside the business (stakeholder orientation) in which the company can flourish.

This is for Conscious leaders. To the extent that free will exists, it is in our conscious choices about our beliefs. We can't choose our biological, physical, or personality makeup; that hand was dealt to us at conception. We mostly can't choose our present circumstances. We did not choose the families we were born into, our socio-economic class, societal norms, or our country and its form of government.

If we are conscious, we choose our beliefs about ourselves, others, and the world in which we live. This is what it means to be an adult, to examine and to not just accept the beliefs of our families and societies. We must consciously decide for ourselves.

In the last decade, the traditionally held theory of evolution has been upended by evolutionary biologist David Sloan Wilson. Wilson (2015) argued that in certain conditions group-level selection is more powerful than individual selection for humans and other social animals. For humans, the survival of the fittest individual is important for evolutionary selection, but it is less important than the health of the group in which they live. If the group fails, then we and our offspring almost certainly fail to survive.

Thinking in terms of survival of the fittest group changes everything. The selfishness that was considered the optimal behavior when we were engaging in a contest of the survival of the fittest individual is no longer the best way to maximize returns for investors. Instead the optimal behavior for maximum shareholder gain (and gain for all of the other stakeholders) is altruism, or prosociality.

The concept is fractal, it works at all levels. At the level of the altruistic individual, employees come to work each day to do what they do best for their group. Their individual talents and perspectives are unique and valued by the group. There is a great deal of autonomy and minimal hierarchy in every work group at every level of the company. Information is freely shared with whomever needs it. Decisions are made where the work is being done and where the information is being generated.

The altruistic group within the company is not a collection of competing individuals. Optimal culture goes way beyond the basic trust level that many companies struggle to achieve. Fear is nonexistent; compassion, generosity, humility, and gratitude are the norm. Each group within the company is highly engaged with the company's higher purpose. Each small group is clear on how it contributes to that purpose and has autonomy to decide how to act.

On a larger scale, the company knows that it is a member of an economic ecosystem and, for it to thrive, the other members of that ecosystem need to be thriving. Altruistic behavior is the norm between companies. Customers and suppliers generously support each other, it is not a matter of getting as much of a limited pie as possible; their generosity actually creates more pie for everyone.

Conscious prosociality and altruism even applies at the planetary level. A planet similar to ours in an alternate universe in which all countries are behaving altruistically will outperform another version of Earth whose nations tolerate selfish nationalist behavior. One might even surmise that in the altruistic universe, climate change and nuclear war will not be looming issues. In the universe that tolerates selfish behavior, the outlook does not look good. We have work to do in our universe, fortunately there is a system for this that works.

A BELL CURVE OF BUSINESSES

Imagine for a moment a bell curve. On one end are the struggling companies with unhappy customers, employees, and suppliers who do not get paid on time. In the middle of the bell curve are all of the companies we generally consider successful. These average companies in the middle deliver acceptable products to their customers and generate reasonable revenue. Their employees fit the Gallup employee survey average of 30 percent engaged, 15 percent actively disengaged, and 65 percent compliant zombie walking through their work day. Most company leaders think this is normal. It is not normal, but unfortunately it is average.

Traditional business practices are keeping the average companies in the middle of the curve and at the same time preventing them from getting to the other far end of that curve. Did you forget about that other extreme end of the curve? The far end where the employees are emancipated, where leadership is fluid, where nearly everyone is fully engaged on a shared mission with a shared purpose, and the customers are so engaged they never consider going anywhere else ....

Movements have sprung up in the last few decades: Conscious Capitalism, Teal Organizations, B Corps, and other similar frameworks. These are not just nicer, more warm and fuzzy ways to do business or new management style options on the business buffet table. Thinking so is a serious misunderstanding. The form of shareholder capitalism that many companies have been practicing and many business leaders have been taught over the last one hundred years or so is dead wrong and badly misaligned with what we know of human nature and objective reality.

Conscious Capitalism, Teal organizations, B Corps, Agile organizations, Lean Manufacturing (when it is done well), and similar systems are well aligned with the knowledge we have recently gained from research in evolutionary biology, positive psychology, and the work of evolutionary psychologists and others. Science backs up these Conscious business operating systems. When we work with the grain of our human natures not only does it feel right, but amazing things happen! Evolution took humans much farther down a collaborative path than it has any other creature, and we have a super power no other creature has: We can create shared reality. The key to a high-performing human organization is the creation of an altruistic shared reality that is aligned with our innate human nature.

This book is in two parts. The first part is the science-y section about us humans: How we function best, what makes us function this way, and why we evolved to do so. I will share with you a simple and cohesive paradigm that you will be able to refer to and apply. The second part is composed of stories about what happened at our company as we implemented the paradigm.

In this book I will take you through the ideas that have most influenced me. These ideas come from positive psychology, evolutionary psychology, genetic psychology, sociology, neurobiology, and evolutionary biology. I love this stuff! It is especially exciting when the pieces all fit so perfectly.

WHO THIS BOOK IS FOR

I expect my audience for this book will probably be people familiar, at least to some extent, with Conscious Capitalism, Teal Organizations, and/or B Corps. You might also be familiar with Agile systems and the principles of Lean Manufacturing. Don't be concerned if you have never heard of any of these things. Familiarity and experience with these things is not at all necessary but may be helpful. I am thrilled for you because a reality-expanding world is about to open up.

Later in the book, once you understand the paradigm, I will describe the four principles of Conscious Capitalism, Conscious Leadership, Conscious Culture, a Stakeholder Orientation, and Higher Purpose; and the Teal Organization framework of "Evolutionary Purpose, Wholeness, and Self Management." I promise it will all make perfect sense.

If you are already a Teal Organization guru, the only twist that I would offer in Frederic Laloux's (2014) Teal Organization paradigm is that I believe a Teal Organization is not so much a step forward to a higher level as a step back into the environment and an optimal way of operating that we humans are "designed" for. Back to those times when our ancestors lived on the African Savanna in small groups with mild hierarchy, egalitarianism, intrinsically rewarding individual contributions, and social lives of their own choosing. This is the way some tribal groups still live today, and how evolutionary psychologists believe our ancestors used to live during the hundreds of thousands of years of evolutionary selection which led to us, specifically, you and me being alive here now. Most of us are not descended from individuals with selfish personalities, or from selfish groups. The groups containing a preponderance of selfish individuals died out. We are the descendants of those who were the altruistic, above average collaborators. It is the success of the altruistic group that ensured those genes that engender altruistic behavior got passed on to us. The genes we carry are responsible for the innate psychological reward systems that motivate us to do the things that promote group performance. We naturally feel good when we do the things that are good for our group.

We are probably the most altruistic humans to walk the planet so far. What we urgently need to do if we and our planet are going to survive is do what we as a species do well and consciously do it even better. We are no longer dispersed groups of tribes. We are controlling the global climate; we have created the anthropocene. We also have the means to destroy each other entirely. We need to recognize that the only path forward lies in altruism and a shared belief in altruism.

What better place to demonstrate this than in business. In our businesses we can create altruistic environments for ourselves and our people who may spend 90,000 hours of their lives working with us. Our companies will measurably outperform the rest, our people will live fulfilling lives, our communities and business eco-systems will thrive, and our planet and our continued existence depend on it.

This book is for the curious. It is for people who have a feeling that the way business is being done by many companies today has a lot of opportunity for improvement. It is for those who need and want a bit more of a nudge to try a different way. It is for those who want to understand the science-based reasons for WHY businesses who apply the principles of conscious business work so well. It is for those who already "get it" but want a firmer foundation of understanding. It is for those who want to understand the underlying principles so they can experiment with business, culture design, and group work practices in a more intentional way. It is for those who dream of a better future and would appreciate some helpful ways to explain this vision to others.

This book is **not** written to convince die-hard shareholder capitalists who believe that people only come to work for a paycheck and that employees have to be carefully "managed" to get any work done. If this sounds like you, consider stopping now. This will be emotionally challenging for you. I am not going to soft pedal these ideas in an attempt to gradually win you over. That would not be fair to the other readers.

I am not going to try to persuade you to create a conscious altruistic business through examples of economic performance of conscious vs regular companies. Others have done that work in the book *Firms of Endearment* (Sisodia et al. 2014, for example), and either you will believe it based on the evidence already provided, or not. There is never going to be a scientifically controlled experiment of two companies in the same market staffed by identical twins (one twin in each company) and equally funded; one that operates in a conscious altruistic way and one that does not, for whom we can compare results over time, much less a replication of that study on more than 100 sets of companies in different industries and countries to prove it beyond a doubt. That is not possible, so if that is the level of proof you seek, be assured you will never find it.

This book is science-based. This is not (as so many business books are) an armchair theory, anecdotal, make-believe, allegorical story, five-step business book complete with pyramids and diagrams. Instead this book is based on my understanding of the last two decades of research in the fields of positive psychology, moral psychology, evolutionary psychology, organizational psychology, genetic psychology, and evolutionary biology, in addition to my personal leadership experience running a company with more than 300 people.

Basing an argument for conscious business on anecdotal evidence, observations, interviews, and market performance benchmarked against other companies is one thing. Basing the argument for conscious business on evolutionary principles and human biology is something else entirely, not only is this a much firmer footing, it also provides insights into what we should be doing in our companies and why these things work.

I am an avid reader of books on psychology, culture, biology, and anything else related to how we humans are designed and motivated and how we can construct our human systems to operate optimally. I am going to include my learnings from other books when they are related to the subject I am covering. They are also part of the basis for my argument. If you prefer you can skip reading the book reflections and go on. If you read the reflections though, you may have a deeper understanding of the points I am making.

I will also include internet links to talks that you may like to click on to get deeper into something or if you need a break from reading and just want to watch something related to the subject at hand while you make dinner.

This book is in two parts. Part one is science focused. Part two is practical application, examples and stories from my personal experience. Feel free to start wherever you want.

TAKING OUT THE TRASH

First, let's take out the trash and baggage of the old systems. We are not rational, self-interested, value-calculating creatures! Nothing good would come of that if we were.

We are driven by our beliefs about ourselves and our world. When our beliefs are confirmed or challenged, our brains generate emotions that may lead to actions. Seldom are we the logical creatures we like to think we are.

There is still a prevailing economic view that humans are rational beings who operate in our own self interest. This neoliberal economic view of humanity has been proven to be utter rubbish.

The theory and the literature it spawned was quite evidently wrong and has been destructive to people and the planet. Scientific research has shown, as I will present here, that we are anything but rational or self-interested. Milton Friedman's (1970) neoliberal business model is on its way to extinction.

WE ARE NOT RATIONAL

Other than our genetic makeup and our present circumstances, neither of which we can control, our behavior is based on two things—our beliefs about ourselves and the world and our brains' continuous predictions of what is about to happen and continuous corrections to those predictions. Our beliefs about ourselves and our world are time and energy shortcuts for our brain. It would be impossible to consider reality objectively in every moment. Instead, based on our beliefs about ourselves, our world, and current circumstances, our brains make predictions and generate actions without our conscious thought. We tend not to engage our rational brain because it is energy intensive and requires mental effort, we tend to run on autopilot. We are unaware of these assumptions and predictive actions going on in our brains. Our emotions and thoughts don't just happen to us. We construct them based on our beliefs about ourselves, others, and the world, and we are capable of consciously changing how we perceive ourselves, the world, and people around us. Emotions emerge from our current view of "reality," our belief systems, and the current expectations our brains create. To change my feeling about something or someone, I need to consciously change my belief.

We do not have brains in order to be rational. If we were objectively observing our environment and making rational decisions, the lion would have killed us already. Evolution could not care less about our brains being rational. Our metabolically expensive brains are designed for our survival and to aid in passing along our genes to the next generation and the generation after that, etc. For some creatures, such as crocodiles, their brains are designed to promote individual self interest. For humans, on the other hand, our individual brains are designed for group-level interest. Humans are group creatures. Our survival and success in passing along our genes generation after generation does not depend on our individual survival as much as it depends on our group's survival. Our brains are therefore "wired" for optimal group performance. Our "rational" brains probably developed to help us explain to other humans why we just did that thing we did in some way that sounds intelligent and well thought out even though it may have been neither. It helps with maintaining status and with group cohesion.

We are not the embodiment of the mythical *homo economicus* of neoliberal economics. We don't have rational brains in order to calculate our next best move for our maximum personal gain. When we are engaging our rational brains, it is most likely because we need to fabricate a logical argument to present to other people to explain *why* we are doing what we emotionally want to and intend to do anyway. (This is the essence of what I gleaned from *The Happiness Hypothesis* by moral psychologist Jonathan Haidt (2006) and his elephant and rider analogy, as well as *71/2 Lessons About the Brain* by neuroscientist Lisa Feldman Barrett (2021).)

WHAT IS A BUSINESS?

Merriam Webster defines business as "a usually commercial or mercantile activity engaged in as a means of livelihood dealings or transactions especially of an economic nature."

This definition, while not incorrect, entirely misses the most important point. The definition describes what it does and how it works, not what a business *is*. This is akin to describing a person as a creature who walks upright, breathes, and consumes food and drink. I think you would agree that though none of that is untrue, that is not really what a person *is*.

A business is a group of people. Yes, they are working together to create something of value.

Their objective intent is to sell the value that they create to their customer in exchange for money. The money allows the company to pay their people a wage, pay their suppliers, and support the community on whom they depend. These financial transactions merely allow the business and its economic ecosystem to continue, just like breathing merely allows you to continue to read this. Are you here to breathe? Making money is only a superficial explanation for what a business is doing and why. There is a lot more going on than the superficial financial transactions because a business is a group of humans, and as we shall see, that can be something quite special. We are capable of very high performance when we get the conditions right, and it feels good when we do.

Even though a business is a group of people, many businesses are not designed with people in mind. Many businesses are designed around the product they are making and the traditional preconceived notions of how a business should be designed and operated. These preconceived notions are good in as far as they actually do help the business to succeed. However, to the extent that the standard business practices get in the way of a high-performing human system, these operating models must be discarded and better human-based systems based on human biology, psychology, and evolutionary principles created to replace them.

Since most businesses are designed without attention to what we now know about people, and because people are the most important part of any business and indeed the primary reason for the existence of the business there is, to put it mildly, a lot of room for improvement.

Here is the paradigm we will end up with:

We act according to our beliefs about ourselves and others. Creating shared worldviews is our super power. An altruistic, purposeful self-view and worldview leads to individual and business success and (bonus points!) happiness. Both at the individual level and the group level.

We have been designed by group-level evolution to be altruistic. Our brains reward us with happiness when we have the autonomy to choose to do the things that benefit our groups.

We are unique individuals and can't help being the unique people that our genes and life experience make us. We need to value that uniqueness; our groups depend on it. Autonomy is the key to releasing this potential and to enabling the intrinsic rewards our brains are designed to give us.

Worldviews and systems that believe and reward us as if we are rational, value calculating, and self-interested are false, destructive and underperforming.

The conscious leader's mission is twofold. To make her workplace and her larger business ecosystem safe for altruism by preventing, correcting, or removing selfish behavior and engendering maximum autonomy and minimal hierarchy.

PART 1

CHAPTER 1

The Problem

U.S. Employee Engagement Trend

	30	28	26	30	28	30	32	33	35 36
26									
18	16	17	15	20	18	18	17	14	13 14

| 2000 | 2002 | 2004 | 2006 | 2008 | 2010 | 2012 | 2014 | 2016 | 2018 | 2020 |

Annual averages
▧ % Engaged   ▧ % Actively disengaged

Note: 2018 results are for January through June

Data Source: "Historic Drop in Employee Engagement Follows Record Rise," Gallup.com.

So what's the problem with the generally accepted current way of doing business?

Each of us will probably spend about 90,000 hours working. That's a lot of time, about one fifth of our lifetime. It is about one third of all the waking hours we will be alive on this planet. If someone spends 90,000 hours disengaged in their work, that is a huge loss in life. Don't we owe our people an engaging work life?

The great thing is, if we get it right, not only will people come to work excited to make a contribution, but they will go home feeling fulfilled. Possibly tired, yes, but fulfilled!

As a bonus for the business, our people will also be more productive. Increased engagement and higher business performance are inextricably linked.

When you look at the Gallup chart above, what do you see? About 30% of people in the U.S. are engaged in what they are doing. About 15% are actively disengaged. The actively disengaged are drilling holes in our proverbial business boat. Some of the holes are even below the waterline.

What the graph does not show is the other 65% of people who are, in my mind, possibly even worse off. These people are not engaged or disengaged. They are just sleepwalking or in a zombie-like state at work, just doing what they are told and getting by. Obedient and compliant wage slaves collecting their paycheck—this is a terrible state to be living in for 90,000 hours of your life.

As much as you might be justifiably angry with the actively disengaged for drilling holes in the group's boat, you have to admit that at least they care about something. They are actively disengaged because something is wrong and they feel it. They are frustrated and acting out, possibly in some sort of passive aggressive way. What they are doing is not constructive, but it shows passion. They are somewhat pissed off, which suggests they feel work should be better than it is. They just don't have a productive way to do something about it. The actively disengaged could be allies for positive change.

CHAPTER 2

Objective and Subjective Reality

Selfishness exists, no one is going to deny that. However altruism also exists and, as we shall see, is much more pervasive than selfishness. We have created a global business culture that insists we prove altruism exists and accepts selfishness as a given. What a strange worldview we have created.

Our belief systems shape what we see. When we believe that selfishness is the way the world works, we are largely blind to the altruism all around us. Seeing selfishness we tend to act more selfishly ourselves. Others act more selfishly in response. When we start to see altruism as the actual way the world works, we begin to see it everywhere and we become more altruistic ourselves.

We made up the concept of capitalism, and we made up the idea of business and how it is done. Because we made it up, we can change it.

To see the business world we have created clearly, we need to take a hard look at reality. We seldom if ever do this. It is a meta state, sort of like thinking about thinking.

Reality comes in two flavors: objective and subjective.

Objective reality is the realm of solid, provable fact. Things like gravity, photosynthesis, the earth is a sphere, and the Krebs tricarboxylic acid cycle (how our mitochondria make energy for our cells) are all facts. Occasionally, our facts change. Previously we thought the earth was flat, but that was disproven and the vast majority of us now accept the earth's spherical shape as fact.

Sometimes objective facts make little difference. You can be a flat-earther and, other than getting teased about it, you will probably not have any issues getting through life. On other objective realities like viruses, vaccines, and wearing masks as protection against viruses, not believing in objective reality can have direct and even lethal consequences for you and others in your group. If the virus happens to mutate inside you into something more lethal and more easily spread, even society at large can be objectively affected by your actions.

Subjective reality is a matter of interpretation; the stuff we make up. It is fiction we create and believe in. To be clear, that does not make it less real. It is subjective reality.

Harry Potter fans will probably recall the scene in the last book, *Harry Potter and the Deathly Hallows* (Rowling 2007), where Harry is having a conversation with Dumbledore in what appears to Harry to be King's Cross station. Harry asks if what he is experiencing is real or if it is just in his head. Dumbledore replies that of course it is in his head "but why on earth should that mean that it is not real?"

One way to illustrate the concept of subjective reality is to use money as an example. Imagine that there is a chimpanzee with a ripe banana. And imagine I have a ten-dollar bill. I offer the ten-dollar bill to the chimpanzee in exchange for the banana, and she looks at me as if I am crazy. Because indeed I am. What chimpanzee in their right mind would exchange a perfectly good, nice, ripe banana for a smelly old piece of wrinkled green paper? Really what a stupid human! If I offer her two ten-dollar bills or even a crisp one hundred dollars, it will make no difference.

If, however, I offer a rumpled and torn five-dollar bill to any cashier in any convenience store anywhere on the planet, they will happily take my five dollars in exchange for a banana or even two bananas any day, also thinking that I am a stupid human but because I am overpaying. Humans are supposed to be smarter than chimpanzees. So what is going on here?

Money is a subjective reality. We invented this idea about 4,000 years ago. Objectively, that ten-dollar bill is just a smelly piece of old paper. But subjectively to most humans, it has higher value. Our currency has value because we believe it does. And because we believe it, it actually does have value. If the majority of us stop believing it, our currency will become worthless bits of paper. This has of course happened numerous times over the last 4,000 years of human history. A currency collapses when a government does, or due to runaway inflation (inflation is just a way of saying we are losing our belief in that currency), or because a country is conquered by another country and its currency becomes worthless.

But it doesn't end with currency. We do this subjective reality thing all the time. It is what Lisa Feldman Barrett (2021), neuroscientist and author of *7 1/2 Lessons About the Brain*, calls our "super power."

Look at how pervasive this fictional stuff is. Other examples? The Norse gods (Odin, Thor, etc.) or really any religion (except the one you believe in, obviously …). This reminds me of Joseph Campbell (2012) chatting with Bill Moyers in their discussion in *The Power of Myth* when Campbell breaks into a chant about old time religion:

OLD TIME RELIGION

We will pray to Aphrodite
She's beautiful but flighty
In her silken see-thru nightie
She's good enough for me.

We will pray to Zarathustra,
Pray just like we used-ta,
I'm a Zarathustra boosta,
He's good enough for me.

We will pray just like the Druids,
Drinking strange fermented fluids,
Go dancing naked through the woods,
They're good enough for me ....

This long list of discarded religions is an example of our super power in action. Creating subjective reality which our group shares. No other creature does this. A good shared subjective reality can give a group coherence and increase collaboration within the group. It is one of the ways we know we are a group and we know what gives us shared meaning and purpose. It allows us to understand what each other is thinking and predict actions because we know we share the same beliefs.

More examples of our ability to create group subjective reality? The divine right of kings. Communism, socialism, democracy, and dare I say it, capitalism itself are all subjective realities. Even basic human rights are a subjective reality. No goddess, god, or gods wrote human rights on a stone tablet and declared it so. We just made it up and believed it, and good thing we did too. Historian Yuval Noah Harari (2015, 116–117) calls these ideas "intersocial subjective reality." Kermit the Frog, singing "Rainbow Connection," was right. These imaginary subjective group ideas can do us a lot of objective good. If you need a light break, you might want to watch Kermit sing this song on YouTube. I bet you will start smiling while listening.

Intersocial subjective realities can also cause a lot of objective harm. Think of all the wars and resulting famine over human history that occurred because of people's deeply held beliefs that propelled them to fight each other. Most of these ideas so desperately fought over are no longer taken seriously by anyone anymore. No Doubt there are wars being fought right now that will seem pointless and ridiculous in 100 years.

Our ability to form a group around a subjective reality can have a dark side. It can cause us to denigrate people from different groups and even treat them as less than human. Many of the current religious and philosophical traditions attempt to avoid this (however successfully) by advocating generosity and caring for strangers and even loving your enemies.

National borders are a subjective reality. Is Ukraine a country or is it part of Russia? It is subjective but very real at the same time.

The divine right of kings was an improvement over the feudal infighting, warring, and pillaging between local warlords. Having a king settles things down, at least within a nation. A king is not going to put up with internal wars because it is costly behavior when viewed from the larger perspective of the kingdom, and it decreases the amount of tribute these former warlords (now vassals who have pledged their fealty) can pay in aggregate to their king.

However, a monarchy also has drawbacks. Individual freedom is not going to be as optimal in a monarchy as it is in a democracy. Feudalism is lacking in upward social mobility options. Once a serf, always a serf.

My reason for bringing up subjective reality is to show that we made up our current view of reality, including business and capitalism. If we made it up, we can change it. There are no objective rules stopping us. When we begin to share the same beliefs about the changes in our group or across society, they become true. This is the only way progress (and unfortunately reverse progress or degeneration) has ever been made.

There was a time when most people knew the earth was flat. Now we know different. Way back in the sixteenth century when we began making up our current ideas about business and capitalism, we did it based on the worldview we had at the time. Next, we will look at the crumbly fictitious foundations of the traditional capitalism system and where these beliefs came from. Then we will look at some newly discovered objective reality (facts) that we did not know when we made up capitalism 1.0.

CHAPTER 3

Using an Evolutionary Lens

*"The world we had been taught to see was alien to our humanness.
We were taught to see the world as a great machine. But then
we could find nothing human in it. Our thinking grew even
stranger—we turned this world image back on ourselves and
believed we too were machines."*
—Margaret Wheatley and Myron Kellner-Rogers (2003)

---

*Exercise: A quick exercise before we go further. You can do this yourself or
better yet, with someone else or a few people either in person or virtually.
If you have some young children available (5–10 years old), that would be
ideal. Make two lists. On one list write everything you can think of that
describes a "Good" person. For example: kind, respectful … etc. Spend a few
minutes making a good long list. When you are done, make a separate list of
qualities of a "Bad" person. We will use these lists later.*

NATURE RED IN TOOTH AND CLAW

Most of us probably remember a class on evolution in high school. We learned that evolution was a process of variation and selection. In any environment, there are different species living in different ecological niches. Whichever species is more suited for the environment would outcompete the others, and one species would gradually displace the others. Outdated species would be replaced by species more suited to the environment.

The same thing happens within a species. There is variation among individuals and those who are stronger, faster, smarter, (sexier), or who excel in some important way in that environment, will outcompete the other individuals, and they will be more successful than others at passing on their genes to descendants.

In this way, those genes that encoded the successful traits get passed on more frequently. You may have read the aptly named book, *The **Selfish** Gene*, by Richard Dawkins (1976) (my emphasis on *selfish*). His book famously looks at this whole evolution thing not on the level of the individual creature who has the gene that makes it more successful, but instead at the level of the "Selfish Gene" being passed along. The gene is "successful" if it gets replicated. It is "competing" with other genes. In Dawkins view, the gene does not care about the other genes or the individuals carrying them. A gene is only selfishly engaged in getting itself passed along.

This all sounds logical. However, if we stay at this level of thinking, it leads to some incorrect assumptions about a bunch of things, including business. This is what happens if we use the survival of the fittest individual or gene-level competition evolutionary lens and apply it to ourselves and to business.

As a human individual, this selfish gene/individual competition view turns life into a competition between ourselves and the people around us. If this model is correct, it leads directly to the self-interested, value-calculating homo economicus praised by the neo liberal school of economics. You may not have heard of this creature before. Homo economicus (economic man) was created in an imaginative "lab" by some economists who needed a simple way to explain what turns out to be their rather dystopian view of reality. They hypothesized that humans are more successful if they act rationally and are concerned only about their own self-interest. More money now, or more money at some point in the future. Making an investment now that rational predictions show are likely to pay off later. Homo economicus is a fictitious, wholly rational creature who calculates value maximization in each situation and opportunity only in terms of self-interest, primarily in terms of financial gain. In this worldview, relationships are transactional and business is purely extractive. According to this worldview, selfishness is good for the individual and good for a business. Magically, as through an invisible hand, this selfish behavior is supposed to turn out wonderfully not only for purely self interested individuals but for everyone in society. It does neither.

The concept is fractal. What it looks like at the small level is essentially the same as it looks at the larger level. What is true at the level of the individual homo economicus is also true at the level of a business populated by them. In this view, a business is a group of homo economicus getting together for enhanced self-interest purposes. Each business is composed of these creatures who work together so long as that collaboration is in their individual self-interest. If it is in their rational self-interest to subjugate another individual, or stab another individual in the back, they do so without hesitation. Predators eat, prey, and compete against other predators. Nothing personal; it's just business.

HINT: Does this sound more like the "Good" person or the "Bad" person you described earlier?

The business in this view is also working only for its own self-interest. The business is owned by shareholders, and therefore, it needs to do whatever is in the self-interest of those shareholders above all else. After all, that is the wholly rational, self-serving reason why each shareholder homo economicus made an investment of their financial capital in it. If the business does not serve this purpose optimally, shareholders withdraw their capital and the business goes bankrupt.

Logically, any individual in the business who profits does so at the expense of the shareholders. There is only so much pie. More pie for me means less for you.

Shareholders grudgingly agree to large bonuses for the CEO and the managers because they recognize fellow homo economicus when they see them. The homo economicus shareholders don't like or feel kinship with these others; they just recognize their utility. They have management skills and can be manipulated with "if/then" financial rewards and bonuses. Logically, in fact, that is the only way to manipulate/incentivize the CEO and management homo economicus. The shareholders know that they can't be there every minute to micromanage the business, so they recognize the practicality of if/then reward bonuses based on economic performance. This is the extrinsically rewarding encouragement that these creatures need to maximize the value produced by everyone else in the organization by whatever legal means necessary. Threats and rewards will be meted out accordingly.

Neoliberal economists expected that these businesses operating in their own self-interest and competing with each other would lead to survival of the fittest businesses and the greatest value creation (for the shareholders and CEO and managers anyway). This was supposed to be good for everyone. Some wealth would inevitably trickle down, wouldn't it?

This is the whole imbecilic worldview promoted by Ayn Rand's (2018) *Atlas Shrugged*.

What a very strange worldview!

If you are ready for a break from reading and would like to watch something related to this, I encourage you to check out this TED Talk on Super Chickens by Margaret Heffernan.

Obviously this neoliberal economic theory has more than a few absurd and fatal flaws. We can acknowledge that some good has come out of this form of capitalism. Capitalism has succeeded marvelously in creating a lot of wealth for a small portion of the population (myself included). Capitalism is teamed up with and is dependent on democracy. Without a peaceful transition of power, there can be no fair laws. Without fair laws, there can be no true capitalism (only crony capitalism). Where capitalism has not been implemented in a completely extractive way, it has created significant value for many if not most other members of a society. So, capitalism in some of its forms has been a good thing.

Billions of people have better lives now than most did decades ago. Capitalism is responsible for some of this. Democracy, human rights, education, and advances in medicine science and technology have also helped. Some of these were aided by business. Some of these prevailed despite business opposition. Most advances are due to the curiosity and generosity of dedicated individuals.

If you feel passionately that capitalism is a disaster, I sympathize with you and I get it, but consider this: If you were about to be reincarnated in a time in human history from the distant past up to today and you have a say in when you are going to be reborn, but not who you would be, where you would be born, the color of your skin, or your economic class, when would you want to be reborn? My guess is that (even with the looming threat of climate change) you would want to be born now. This is the progress we have made. Capitalism is not responsible for all of that progress; democracy, science, and education are other important parts of that mix. Business can be done imperfectly and can cause harm but when done well, it produces significant good.

We made it up, so we can make it better!

There is, to say it lightly, *a lot* of room for improvement in the way business is generally done. The traditional view assumes scarcity; there is only so much pie to be had, so if I get a larger slice, you will be getting a smaller one. But what if we can create more pie for everyone? What if we can all live within the boundaries of what the planet can sustain and still be better off than we are now? What if we can live not just sustainably, what if we can live in a generous way with each other and the planet? Is there another way?

CHAPTER 4

Group-level Selection

EVOLUTION 2.0

When Darwin (2019) wrote *On the Origin of Species*, he knew nothing of modern genetics. He had noticed that in nature there was variation and selection, and he inferred some sort of heritable replication process for the adaptations that worked well in that environment. He also noticed that though this theory explained a lot, there were some things that were difficult to explain. How to account for altruistic behavior, for example? Why would one creature show compassion and generosity to another? It might make selfish-gene sense when an individual is generous to a genetic relative. But how could compassion or generosity to a stranger ever be rational?

There is a cynical explanation that by being generous I am showing that I have excess resources, that I can afford to share my resources, which could be a way of signaling to a prospective mate that I am stronger and better off than most and therefore more desirable. Or maybe I do you a favor now, so that you will be in my debt, and I can get you to do something for me in return later. A quid pro quo, crony capitalism, mafioso godfather contract worldview.

When you have done an altruistic favor for someone, it is far more likely that none of this entered your mind. You did no rational self-interest calculations. A rational thought may in fact have never entered your brain. It is more likely that it simply felt good or right to act that way. Your self-view, beliefs about that person, and beliefs about your group norms and social relationships, resulted in your altruistic behavior.

As we will see, generosity is in fact dangerous if we are living in an environment of selfishness. However, if our environment is altruistic, generosity will be well received and will perpetuate the altruistic behavior of others. Altruistic groups outperform selfish groups. Therefore, altruism and generosity is the correct and most beneficial behavior when we take care to create and maintain the right group conditions that eliminate selfish behavior, making it safe for altruism.

This is a key to understanding why conscious businesses perform so well. Their cultures are based on dependable altruistic behaviors. When people sense they are in an altruistic environment, they respond generously; they freely contribute initiative and creativity. However, when people believe they are in a selfish environment, they only contribute what is required (quiet quitting) and what can be extrinsically motivated by bribes (bonuses) or threats. They will only be obedient and compliant and maintain skill levels to the extent that they are extrinsically manipulated into doing this. This is obviously going to lead to a huge differential in company performance.

GROUP-LEVEL SELECTION

There have been advances in evolutionary thought over the last few decades. There was a big debate in evolutionary biology circles over group-level evolution and whether it was really a thing. It seems like a silly debate now, but eventually it was decided that group-level selection is a valid evolutionary path. It is a simple shift, but it changes everything. What if the selfish gene is not the whole story? What if it is not really the survival of the fittest individual that determines our success at passing along our genes? What if evolution happens at the level of the group instead of at the level of the individual or the gene? As it turns out, evolution has used this group strategy over and over again. It is all around us, and yet we usually don't see it until it is pointed out.

WHY DO PEOPLE GO TO WORK?

Exercise: Take a few moments and do this exercise. The conclusions you draw from this material will be more meaningful if they are based on your ideas. Better still, do this with a partner or a small group of people you like. Come up with as many reasons for the question "Why do people go to work?" as you can. As an idea and mental prompt, consider why your parents went to work, your aunts and uncles. Someone you admire. Your kids, if you have them and they have jobs. Why does Iron Man go to work? To be fair to the DC universe, why does Wonder Woman go to work? Come up with as many answers as you can. The more answers and the greater the variety of reasons the better.

Billions of years ago, the oceans contained only single-cell organisms. They replicated by dividing into two cells. For millions of years, each cell went its own way. At some point, though, a couple of sister cells who split stayed together. There was an evolutionary advantage of some sort. Maybe it was just because in combination they were larger, so it was much harder for another single-cell organism to "eat" them. Over time they evolved to form collaborative groups and, though they contained the same genes, the cells developed differently and performed different functions. The result is multicellular organisms. Over millions of years of mutation, variation, environmental selection, and replication, creatures evolved. Mitochondrial cells created energy for the host cell. Some cells specialized in digestion, some grew little wriggly things that served as propulsion, some became light sensing and eventually eyes, and some became a nervous system to send and receive messages between the cells.

We are an example of these multicellular organisms. Each of us is composed of billions of cells. Each of those cells is built according to and contains the same set of our unique DNA. These cells are not all the same however. Each of them is different and is fulfilling a different function. Each of our cells is working in the service of our whole selves. Our heart muscle cells are pumping to circulate oxygen and nutrients to the other cells in our bodies through blood cells. Our lungs pass the CO_2 out of our red blood cells and replace it with oxygen. Diaphragm muscles contract and expand, moving the air in and CO_2 out. Our liver, kidneys, and digestive system all have different cells working together in collaboration to perform their unique functions. Our immune system's white blood cells willingly sacrifice themselves to keep out intruders. Our brains, which use twenty percent of our body's energy (our most expensive organ to operate), are managing this incredible, complex, harmonious symphony. This is, in fact, the main job of our brains.

What happens if some of these cells decide to act like the mythical homo economicus of neoliberal economics? What if they begin to act only in their own self-interest? What if they take more resources than they give back? What if they multiply at the expense of other cells? We have a word for this: cancer.

Multicellular organisms are an example of group-level selection. There are more and stranger examples though. Siphonophores are creatures that live in the deep oceans. They can grow to hundreds of feet long. They look like jellyfish, possessing a bell that pulses to propel them along and tentacles trailing behind. Unlike most multicellular organisms, their cells do not contain the same DNA. They are a collaborative group of different organisms working together. The bell is one organism, the tentacles another, and the digestive system a third. They are working together to support each other in a symbiotic relationship.

You are probably familiar with other types of symbiotic organisms like lichen, which is a combination of a fungus and an algae. Or coral reefs, which are coral polyps and algae living in a collaborative relationship. When corals get too warm, they expel their algae and eventually die.

Of course, there are a lot of animals that live in groups. Schools of fish, flocks of birds, herds of horses, packs of wolves, pods of whales, a dazzle of zebras, a bouquet of skunks (just kidding about the skunks).

Some primates like chimpanzees, bonobos, baboons, and ourselves live in collaborative groups. We are by far the best collaborators of the bunch. Interestingly, chimpanzees, as smart as they are, don't easily get the idea that an experimenter is trying to help them. Dogs are much "smarter" than chimps in this regard, and therefore, take cues from the experimenter and succeed in the identical task at nearly 100 percent vs the chimps at just over 50 percent. Our natural friendliness, like that of dogs, has been bred into us by our own self-domestication. Our friendliness (altruism) is the basis for our success as a species. For more on this read *Survival of the Friendliest* by Brian Hare and Vanessa Woods (2020).

What does group-level selection look like and how does it work? What is the variation and selection and replication system? In what way is it encoded in our genes? On what levels is it happening? Is it purely genetic?

Imagine two "human" groups. One resembles a group of fictitious homo economici and the other is a group of real humans. They are confronted with a threat or an opportunity. How does it play out?

The group of homo economici is attacked by a rival band. Each individual in the group rushes to gather up their own possessions and runs away. Everyone, especially the weaker individuals, is left to fend for themselves as best they can. Some homo economici see how it is going to play out and conclude that "their side" is going to lose the fight. Seeing this they join the rival band and begin stealing from former "friends." Individuals who are injured are left to die of their injuries or become prey of wild animals.

Now imagine a group of real humans is attacked by a rival band. They gather together to protect each other. Weaker individuals are guarded by stronger individuals who selflessly take positions around the perimeter of the weaker group. Stronger members take risks of bodily harm to protect the others without a rational thought of 'what's in it for me' entering their minds. They just do it. Even individuals who joined the group only a week ago and share no family ties or genetic reasons for protecting each other risk their lives for the other members of what has become their group. By uniting, they are able to repel the attack and, after the conflict, they take care of each other, caring for injuries and sharing their food.

Or, consider this mental scenario:

1. Salmon are running in the stream nearby. One of the homo economici discovers this. They catch fish easily out of the stream and sit there enjoying a personal feast. Only when they are full do they even have a passing thought of telling

any of the others about the salmon run. This is just too much bother though. It would take at least 15 minutes to get back to camp to tell them. They will probably show up sooner or later to get a drink and see it for themselves. Why am I even thinking about them anyway? If they are just too dumb to figure it out for themselves, serves them right. My stomach is full and the sun is warm, time to take a nap.

vs.

2. Salmon are running in the stream nearby. Young friends playing near the stream notice all the fish. They call out to each other excitedly and immediately run back to the camp to tell the others. When they get back to the camp and share the news, the best fishermen immediately gather their gear and head to the stream, the little ones leading them all full of excitement and eager to watch and help. With a few small discussions and no direction given from anyone in particular, the camp is packed up and moved to an open space near the stream. Some people get started on building fish-drying racks and fish-smoking fires. By evening they are ready for a shared feast. There is singing, dancing, and storytelling. A few days later they meet members of another tribe. They want to share in their bounty so they invite the other tribe to join them by the stream. They share stories and make new friendships. They devise and learn new fishing techniques from each other. They trade with each other and make generous gifts of precious items to newfound friends. Over the next few days, they cure and dry enough fish to feed themselves for weeks.

It is obvious that the real humans will outcompete the imaginary homo economici. The reason for their success is human altruism and mutual collaboration. Group-level altruism and cooperation will beat selfish groups and selfish individuals every time. The trick is to have a way to eliminate selfish behavior in the group. If some individuals persist in selfish behavior, send them packing. This is where Prosocial Core Design Principles (Atkins, Wilson, and Hayes 2019) come in.

> "Selfishness beats Altruism within groups. Altruistic groups beat selfish groups. All else is commentary" (Wilson 2007, 345).

Watch this YouTube video featuring David Sloan Wilson and Robert Sapolski Extending Darwin's Revolution:

You can start twelve minutes in if you prefer to not watch the whole thing.

I am inserting a book reflection here. If you follow it, you will get a deeper, more expanded view of the concept of Prosocial Core Design Principles. It might also provide a break. Ideally you will be inspired to read these books.

BOOK REFLECTION

This View of Life: Completing the Darwinian Revolution by David Sloan Wilson (2019)

How are we going to get through this pandemic? How are we going to put this country together again? How are we going to ameliorate racial and financial inequality? How are we going to collaborate globally to deal with climate change? How are we going to deal with the next global crisis after that?!! We can be sure there will be more, and we need to develop our skills and be capable of dealing with them effectively.

David Sloan Wilson is an evolutionary biologist. His book *This View of Life* has an answer.

It is what he calls the third way. The third way is based on his work in evolutionary biology and Elinor Ostrom's "Core Design Principles" for successful human groups.

Ostrom is the Nobel Prize-winning scientist who studied groups that did not have a tragedy of the commons. They managed their water resources or their fisheries effectively and sustainably. She found that there were eight key principles embodied by these groups. She called them "Core Design Principles."

This book is about a whole lot more than this, but I am pulling this nugget out because it seems the most relevant now.

I sometimes think it is just going to be too hard to put this country back together so maybe we should just split up and go our separate ways. Unfortunately we can't afford to do that. In fact we need to develop even stronger relationships within our country and between all nations if we are going to succeed as a species. We will not overcome this pandemic unless everyone on the planet works together. Same goes for all of the other major crises we face now and in the future.

Laissez-faire does not work. We see this in capitalism run amok. Selfish individuals taking too much. Cancerous, homo economicus behavior. Financial inequality.

Central control (i.e., communism) does not work either. It is too slow to respond and the world is too complex. (Many large corporations try to run themselves through tight central control. Information travels up and approvals travel down the chain of command and, instead of being agile, they are slow and ponderous.)

What does work is what David Sloan Wilson calls a third way. A society (or a company) based on his and Ostrom's (2010) Prosocial Core Design Principles.

There are eight of them. Here they are in brief:

Strong group identity and understanding of purpose

Proportional equivalence between benefits and costs

Fair and inclusive decision-making

Monitoring agreed upon behaviors

Graduated sanctions

Fast and fair conflict resolution

Local autonomy

Polycentric governance (Groups of Groups within Groups)

For a more complete description of the Prosocial Core Design Principles read *Prosocial: Using Evolutionary Science to Build Productive, Equitable, and Collaborative Groups* (Atkins, Wilson, and Hayes 2019, 24).

Here are my thoughts on the design principles through the lens of a conscious company or B-orp:

1. Employees are proud and passionate about their work. They know they are a group, and they know the mission, their Higher Purpose.

2. People are paid generously and are appreciated for their work. It is not a work-life balance thing. Work itself is fulfilling.

3. People are included in decision-making. Stakeholders' interests are represented when decisions are made, not after the fact as window dressing and greenwashing.

4. Employees care about and monitor their company's performance in areas of social responsibility. They monitor behavior within the organization to make sure it is consistent with their principles.

5. When there is a perceived transgression of principles, people first of all inquire and then, if needed, gently remind the individuals involved before escalating. Most people want to do the right thing and just need a gentle reminder. They may even be unaware of the inconsistency in what they did.

6. When things get out of hand, when transgressions escalate within the company or within the company's economic ecosystem, people respond quickly and fairly to fix the problem. This could mean disciplinary action, demotions, dismissals, or ceasing to do business with another company. If the problem is not addressed, people will become demoralized.

7. People and groups have autonomy in how they get their work done. Trust your people to find new solutions and to try them. The more experiments we run the better. Individuals and groups should get advice from those who are knowledgeable and who will be effected by the changes. The bigger the change the more advice should be sought.

8. Individuals and groups join forces on the same mission. Whether they are suppliers, customers, or competitors does not matter. It is the mission that is critical. Even our competitor is our partner when we are working to solve the same issue.

This works on all levels. It works on the level of a small group of five people working together. It also works on a global level.

What is good for my country may not be good for the global community and environment.

At what level are we engaged? Are we being selfish for ourselves, our company, our nation, or are we putting the good of the whole larger group first?

Here is what I think it looks like through the climate change lens:

Our group is all of humanity. Climate change due to human behavior is a fact. We have only one planet, one ecosystem, and we have to protect it. This is the mission. Everything else comes after this.

We need to treat each other fairly. Economically, racially, etc. This needs to go into our decision-making on how we address the crisis.

We need to be democratic. We need to hear each other out. We need to respectfully discuss the issues and share ideas based on factual evidence. Where there is no evidence, we need to get it ASAP. The planet's voice is the main voice we are representing and hearing from.

We will monitor each other. We will agree on what will be effective solutions to the climate crisis and what we will do.

When we fall short, others will first gently remind us of our responsibility and what we agreed to do. (This happens at all levels, from the level of the individual right up to the level of a nation.)

If there are repeated and severe violations (at any level), there are swift and measured pre-agreed upon consequences and solutions.

Allow autonomy to achieve goals in the way the local community thinks best. The more experiments we run, the more good solutions we will discover and the more we can refine them. We realize that complex issues cannot be solved by central control. They require diverse experimentation.

We are all in this together. Our generation may not see much in the way of benefits for ourselves, but future generations will be depending on us to do the right thing for them NOW.

I am sure you can see now how this can be applied to racial justice, economic inequality, the pandemic, and putting our country together again.

I can't help myself, so I will go on a bit more.

"In the long history of humankind (and animal kind, too) those who learned to collaborate and improvise most effectively have prevailed" (Darwin 1859/2019).

I want to point out that doing things to disenfranchise people, or to make it difficult for them to vote is a violation of CDP number three, fair and inclusive decision-making.

I think it is also worth mentioning that some people have been observed fostering misinformation that "the election was stolen," CDP number four, monitoring behavior.

These people have been gently reminded that continuing to sow misinformation about the last election is a violation of our republic's democratic principles, which rely on truth and justice. If they continue to persist, sanctions must be escalated, CPD number five, up to and including being removed from the group (imprisonment). Free speech is one thing; we are free to share our opinion. Denying a fact in order to overthrow the government, participating in and encouraging sedition, is not freedom of speech it is lying. When lying causes harm to others the lyars must be held accountable for the harm they have caused.

If these misinformers persist in these transgressions, the result must be a swift, just, and definitive response to that behavior if our country is going to be effective for its people and for our republic's continued existence. CDP number six, fast and fair conflict resolution. If the justice department does not hold people accountable for the attack on the capitol, including the people in government who actively encouraged it, and do it quickly, this CDP will not be met and our country's continued existence will be imperiled. Justice delayed is justice denied.

CHAPTER 5

The Key to Life (and Group Success) is Happiness

How do we know we can trust each other? How do we know that others care about us and will willingly go out of their way to help us out?

Let's look at human motivation. If you did the exercises on describing good and bad people and answered the question about why people go to work you already have the answers. If you did not do the exercises, it's not too late. You can take a break and do them now. The benefit of doing them is that they will be your ideas and not ideas contaminated by me.

WHY DO PEOPLE *REALLY* GO TO WORK?

Let's look at the answers you came up with for this question. You can categorize them into one of two different things. As many philosophers have observed over time, people want two things: They want to avoid pain and suffering, and they want to find happiness.

In the avoiding pain and suffering category are a paycheck, food, clothing, shelter/rent, health insurance, and a 401K retirement plan to avoid pain and suffering in the future. Possibly you go to work to avoid the wrath of your spouse for goofing off and going fishing.

There are two very different parts to the finding happiness half of what we all want. In the first part are all the extrinsically rewarding things: a fancier car or larger house, a new cell phone or a large screen TV, even a luxury vacation or cruise.

In the second part of the finding happiness category are the intrinsically rewarding things. Things like relationships, learning new things, enjoying the work itself/engagement, having some fun, and sharing what you do well with a group you care about. Teaching others what you know. To work on something with a higher purpose. To do meaningful work in service of others.

I am sure you have things in each of these categories in your lists. A homo economicus would only have items from the "avoiding pain and suffering" and the "extrinsic rewards" on their lists.

Most HR departments consider only these two categories when creating a job offer. These HR departments are totally missing the point of work.

For humans, the intrinsic rewards are the most important. We will very willingly earn a lower rate of pay, and forgo a fancier car or a luxury cruise, to work on something that we are highly skilled in, want to learn, or that serves a higher purpose with a group of people we care about and who care about us.

That being said, we will not put up with unfairness. If I know that I could earn twice the salary at a different company with a cut-throat homo economicus culture, I will not leave my group for the extra money because my job is meaningful and I feel like an essential part of my group. I will, however, be quite pissed off if I find that someone within my own company, who is just as good as I am and essentially doing my same job, is earning twice as much as I am. This is a natural reaction to unfairness.

To see it in action, check out this YouTube Video.

This sort of unfairness hurts in two ways. First, it is just unfair, as the two capuchin monkeys demonstrated in the video above. Second, when this happens in a group, it is a betrayal of essential group norms. It suggests a dysfunctional group that I either need to see fixed or I might leave it. In accordance with Prosocial CDP number two, there must be *proportional equivalence of benefits and costs.* If one monkey gives the researcher a rock and gets a cucumber and the other monkey gives the researcher a rock and gets a grape, that is just not proportional equivalence for the work done.

If an individual or group within the larger group acts selfishly, that is exactly like cancer cells that are consuming resources and not contributing to the group as they should. In a human group, we call this unfair; in an organism it is cancer. The group's immune system must be on alert for selfish behavior and eliminate it.

So, if intrinsic rewards are the most important motivators for humans, is there other evidence for the power of intrinsic rewards and how they work? Yes, quite a lot actually.

The field of positive psychology has been studying what makes us happy for the last two decades. This is not light, fluffy research but serious stuff. Hypotheses are proposed and rigorously tested.

Peer-reviewed articles are published and studies are replicated with consistent results.

Martin Seligman is considered the father of positive psychology. When he was elected president of the American Psychological Association in 1996, he observed that psychology had done a lot of work studying and discovering treatments for depression, anxiety, and other psychological issues. Psychology had done a fairly good job of making life better for a relatively small percentage of people who had been suffering. This was good, worthwhile work, and psychology should rightfully be proud of what had been accomplished. Seligman had been noticing something else though, when looking at a large sample of people, there were those who were doing very poorly, the majority who were more or less average, and those few who were doing exceptionally well. A typical bell curve. Psychology had been fairly successful moving the people who suffered the most up under some of the larger part of the bell into the average zone. This is good work, to be sure.

However, psychology had not been studying those who were doing extraordinarily well. What can we learn from studying extraordinary cases that we can share with the average majority to increase their level of fulfillment and move them closer to the level of the extraordinary?

Seligman writes in his 2011 book, *Flourish*, that there are five reliable ingredients to happiness, human well-being, and human flourishing: Positive Emotion, Engagement, Relationships, Meaning, and Achievement (PERMA, if you like mnemonics).

Another positive psychology researcher, Sonjya Lyubomirski (2007), shares the results of her research and the research of others in her book *The How of Happiness*. She explains that human happiness has three distinct components. The first part is worth fifty percent of our happiness and unfortunately there is not much we can do about it. It turns out that fifty percent of our happiness is heritable. It is genetic. We all know some people who are more like Christopher

Robbin's Eeyore and some who are more like Tigger. Because of the genetic cards we have been dealt, we all fall somewhere on this continuum and to some extent, we simply can't help where we landed.

But what about the other fifty percent?

About ten percent of our happiness is situational. This part lives in "if/then" statements. We spend a lot of time thinking about this part. If only I had a nicer car. When this pandemic is over and I can go on that luxury cruise, then I will be happy. If only I earned about forty percent more, then I would be happy. (It turns out that forty percent more than whatever we are earning now is the magic number we think will make us happy. At least until we get accustomed to it and then we need another forty percent bump.) Even though we have some control over our present circumstances, it is limited.

So two out of three down, one is genetic, one is situations largely out of our control, and still one to go. We have another forty percent of our happiness pie to work with. What is it?

Lyubomirski says there are twelve things we can do for sustained happiness. We don't need to do them all. Some will feel more suited to us than others. The key is to pick one or two and continue to do them on a regular basis. Like exercise, you need to keep it up.

They are gratitude, cultivating optimism, avoid overthinking and social comparison, acts of kindness, relationships, coping strategies, forgiveness, living in the present/flow, savoring joy, authentic goals, religion and spirituality, body care: exercise and meditation.

Let's use gratitude as an example. As Lyubomirski writes, expressing gratitude on a regular basis is a meta strategy for sustained happiness. How should I go about doing it? Well as Grandma probably told you, you can count your blessings. Good advice, Grandma! But we can do better. For maximum effect, the research shows, we should express gratitude about once a week. You could write some thank-you notes or express gratitude with a gratitude partner. Like jogging with a partner, working together will keep you going, and you will get more out of it by hearing the things your partner is grateful for this week. Can we do better still? You bet. Optimally, we should express gratitude to the people we spend time with or work with or who has done something we are grateful for. Speaking directly to the person you feel gratitude toward is better. Doing it in a group you care about is better still.

My son told me of a practice that fits this bill perfectly. He was part of a LARP (Live Action Role Play) group. It is a combination of cosplay and improvisational theater, and the group is its own audience. This group gets together once a week. Each person develops a character and interacts with the others in character. Before it starts, there is a basic description of the tension-generating issue and the setting. Then actors begin interacting in character.

At the end of each weekly session, the group gathers in a circle and participants can share something they particularly enjoyed, such as how someone had done something really well. Not everyone gets a compliment every time, but occasionally each participant does. Regardless, the process became a fulfilling part of his week. You can find his full description of this practice in Part 2.

This LARP example of a gratitude round is intrinsically rewarding to all who participate in it or witness it. Seligman and Lyubomirski's lists are both pointing to the same human intrinsically rewarding things. These intrinsically rewarding human behaviors make us authentically and sustainably fulfilled and happy as long as we continue to engage in them and practice them. We are spending 90,000 hours working, and work is a great place to practice them. Intrinsic rewards are also the critical things that make our groups highly functioning. Without these, our groups underperform and we feel miserable. Intrinsically rewarding human activity is essential for us and for our groups but missing or minimal in so many work environments.

If you would like to read my reflection on Lyubomirsky's book, *The How of Happiness*, here it is below:

BOOK REFLECTION

The How of Happiness: A New Approach to Getting the Life You Want by Sonja Lyubomirsky (2007)

Lyubomirsky is a professor and researcher at the University of California, Riverside.

All human beings want to avoid pain and suffering and find happiness. How do we find happiness? This book has about twenty years of scientific research around finding sustainable authentic happiness.

In her book she shares her research and the research of others in the field of positive psychology. Sustained authentic happiness does not mean that you can do something once and be happy forever, it means that if you continue to practice these things, you will continue to maintain a higher level of happiness.

There are three contributing factors to our happiness.

Our present circumstances. Did you just get a puppy? Did your cat die last week? Did someone unfriend you on Facebook? These are the somewhat random things that happen to us that we spend a lot of time obsessing about. We think, *If only I had this pair of shoes, or if only that person would* … then I would be happy. These things account for only ten percent of our overall happiness. We need to spend less time on these things. A new big-screen TV will make us happier for a while, but that happiness will quickly fade.

DNA. Our genetic coding is responsible for a whopping fifty percent of our happiness (at least fifty percent of our personality also but that is another book). We all live on a spectrum and have a happiness setpoint we naturally gravitate back to. This is called hedonic adaptation. We all know some people who are like Tigger, they bounce out of bed in the morning and are ecstatically happy nearly all the time. We also know people like Eeyore. They could have won the lottery yesterday, but today paying the taxes on their winnings is all they can think about. These people can't help the DNA hand they have been dealt and neither can we. Just recognizing the impact of our DNA and accepting ourselves for who we are is the best we can do on this.

The good news is that the remaining forty percent of our happiness is within our control. This forty percent is what the book is about.

Lyubomirsky provides proven strategies for sustained authentic happiness: gratitude, cultivating optimism, avoid overthinking and social comparison, acts of kindness, relationships, coping strategies, forgiveness, living in the present / flow experience, savoring life's joys, authentic goals, religion and spirituality, care of your body, and meditation.

As she explains, not all of these are for everyone. She suggests that you just try the ones that feel right for you.

She goes into each one in depth. She shares the research and findings and her own experience.

As an example, here is a quick look at gratitude.

Due to the exhaustive, exacting research, we know that practicing gratitude really works. However, research shows that, while writing a gratitude list is good, we can do better. Ideally we should not count our blessings every day. The optimal frequency for most people is once a week. Furthermore, it's better to do this with a gratitude partner, someone who you team up with (like an exercise partner). You each collect things you are grateful for over the week and then share them with each other.

Better still is a Gratitude Round, a practice we began in our maintenance department years ago. Each Friday morning, after we had discussed the plans for the day, about ten mechanics and I would do a Gratitude Round. There was no pressure and it was entirely optional (I explained how it is generally done and I held the space open for it to happen). All of these intrinsically rewarding things need to be "opt in," or they do no good. There is no intrinsic reward without the autonomy to participate or not.

Sure, it can feel a bit awkward at first, but someone will start and others will also speak up. Eventually the awkwardness fades and it becomes a thing that people look forward to.

People who wanted to could thank someone else in the group for something they did during the week. Maybe someone shared their knowledge. Maybe someone gave a helping hand, or brought in a birthday cake, or cleaned the shop, or reorganized the parts, or accomplished a particularly difficult job for the first time. This weekly practice took just a few minutes but gradually changed the dynamic among mechanics. People became more generous with their knowledge and looked out for each other more. Our work community became more caring. People would freely volunteer to try and fix something they had no prior experience with (psychological safety). Others would quickly share tips or volunteer to help out in case they got stuck.

We did other gratitude-related things, too. We had a "Compliments and Accomplishments" white board in the lunch room so that people could write a note to thank someone for something or to share an improvement that had been made.

Any other sources of wisdom on intrinsic rewards, authentic human fulfillment and sustained happiness?

In 2016, the Dalai Lama, Archbishop Desmond Tutu, and Douglas Abrams (a Buddhist, a Christian, and a Jew!) authored a book called *The Book of Joy*. Drawing from philosophical and spiritual traditions thousands of years old, they share eight pillars of happiness which are remarkably similar to Sonjya Lyubomirski's recommendations for sustained happiness.

The eight pillars of joy are: perspective, acceptance, humility, humor, forgiveness, compassion, gratitude, and generosity. I recommend reading their book. Some of these pillars will be fairly self-explanatory, though perspective and acceptance could use some clarification. By Acceptance, the authors don't mean giving up. Acceptance is recognizing when your current strategy toward your goal is not working. The Dalai Lama says that, if you have a worthy goal, you should never give up. However you need to know when to try a different strategy.

Perspective is a consciously chosen outlook on life. The authors share a story of two soldiers who suffer essentially the same injury during combat. Both lose their legs. A few days later, one of them is lying in bed in a fetal position wishing he had died. He is totally inconsolable, despite the best efforts of the nurses. At the same time, the other soldier is in a wheelchair being pushed along through a garden by one of the nurses. He notices the beautiful spring flowers, which are now at eye level due to his new position in a wheelchair. He is overcome with gratitude that he survived and will soon see his wife and children.

Let's delve some more into perspective here because it is quite profound. We have already discussed how we humans are not really all that rational. We are motivated to a great extent by our emotions. But where do these emotions come from? Do they just happen as some people suggest, or do they come from someplace we have some control over?

Our brains are prediction organs. That's the brain's main job. If we waited for something to happen to figure out what to do, it would be too late. Instead, our brains are continually framing up what is likely going to happen next and getting us ready for it. Our brains then make continual adjustments as events unfolds. Much of the "reality" we perceive is constructed by our brains before it happens.

We have beliefs or constructs that determine our feelings and responses. The Dalai Lama calls these "perspectives" about ourselves and our world. When things are unfolding according to our notions of ourselves in our world (our brains' predictions based on our perspective), we may have a positive emotional response. When things are not unfolding as our perspective predicts, our brains give us an emotional response to get our attention. That is the purpose of emotions. Controlling emotions is possible but difficult. Consciously choosing our perspective is easier and more likely to work.

When we change our self-view or worldview, we will no longer have the same emotional response to the same situation. How well are your belief systems working for you?

My college psychology professor at Fairfield University, Dr. John McCarthy, said many times, "People act the way they do because of the way they view themselves and view the world. If you want to change someone's behavior, you need to become a significant other (someone whose perspective they trust). You then need to offer them information contrary to their self-view or worldview that is not too emotionally charged and at a rate they can handle. If you offer information that is too emotionally charged or at a rate they can't handle, they will first reject the information and if you persist, they will reject you."

We are capable of doing this for ourselves as well as for others. We can consider information about ourselves and our world that is contrary to or different from our current beliefs and decide to adopt it. That's perspective.

For a neurobiological perspective on perspective, we can turn to neurobiologist Lisa Feldman Barrett. In this TED talk, she explains how our brains work and how we are the "architects of our experience."

> ## BOOK REFLECTION
>
> ### *The Book of Joy: Lasting Happiness in a Changing World* by the Dalai Lama and Desmond Tutu, with Douglas Abrams (2016)
>
> This book is set in the framework of two great friends, the Dalai Lama and Archbishop Desmond Tutu, getting together, possibly for the last time. Douglas Abrams knits the narrative together as they share their wisdom with characteristic humility and humor.
>
> They draw a distinction between the superficial happiness of external things and deep joy. If happiness is reliant on external circumstances, it is not true joy. Joy is the happiness that comes from inside us, from our choice of perspective, and from intrinsic rewards.
>
> Desmond Tutu (page 5) describes his belief in what he calls "self-corroborating truth," when different fields of knowledge point to the same conclusion. Indeed when positive psychology and evolutionary psychology point to the same truth as millennia-old Christian and Buddhist spiritual traditions, and timeless philosophies, we are most likely on the right track.
>
> Self-corroborating truth gets me excited. I see these same connections between this book and many others that I have read, which should be no surprise; these books are all accurate expositions of human biological and social systems.
>
> *When asked by a young waitress about the meaning of life:*
>
> *"The Dalai Lama answered immediately. "The meaning of life is happiness." He raised his finger, leaning forward, focusing on her as if she were the only person in the world. "Hard question is not, 'What is meaning of life?' That is easy question to answer! No, hard question is what make happiness. Money? Big house? Accomplishment? Friends? Or …" He paused. "Compassion and good heart? This is question all human beings must try to* •

answer: What make true happiness?" He gave this last question a peculiar
emphasis and then fell silent, gazing at her with a smile.

"Thank you," she said, "thank you." She got up and finished stacking
the dirty dishes and cups, and took them away."

Slate Feb 26, 2014

There are eight pillars of joy described in the book: perspective,
humility, humor, acceptance, compassion, generosity, and gratitude.
They are very similar to the things that Sonja Lyubomirsky (2007)
describes in her book *The How of Happiness* as the essential things that,
if practiced, on a regular basis lead to true lasting happiness.

From an evolutionary psychology perspective, we are descended
from ancestors who lived in highly collaborative groups. (The non
collaborative were less successful evolutionarily and died out.) Can
you imagine a group of people working effectively together without
humility, humor, forgiveness, compassion, generosity, or gratitude?
Think about it for a minute and try to imagine it. Leave out just one
of these pillars of joy, and a human group would be in serious trouble.

Turn the question around and imagine a group abundantly full
of these things. How much would you want to be part of that group?
How successful would that group probably be?

Evolution has baked these pillars of joy into us. When we do generous things or we express gratitude to someone, our brains produce
an intrinsic feeling of joy as a reward. We feel joy when we are compassionate, when we see someone else being compassionate, and even
when we hear about an act of compassion because compassion was and
still is essential for our group survival. It is our true human nature.
These eight pillars of joy bring us together. When our group lacks
these, we feel uncomfortable and may leave that group.

The first pillar is perspective. This is about how we choose to
view ourselves in our world, it is related to our awareness of our Purpose. In addition to the eight pillars of joy, there are of course other

things that are intrinsically rewarding, like learning and teaching, for example.

This year has highlighted the issue: When our chosen perspective places not wearing a mask as an individual right and freedom that is more important than human compassion and generosity, compassion for exhausted healthcare workers, and people who are not in good health, it leads to suffering and catastrophic human loss. Our ancestors were successful because they put the larger group's needs ahead of their personal and family's desires.

If we continue down the path of material goals, extrinsic rewards, and selfishness, not only will we be following a path of destruction, we will not find the joy in life that is waiting there for us.

If we humans are going to make it for the next thousand years or so, it will be due to our practice of these eight pillars of joy and the other intrinsically rewarding things that make us truly human. It will be because we put compassion and generosity before selfishness. If our descendants are here one thousand years from now, it will be because we learned to put the needs of all humanity and our planet ahead of our own desires, our tribe's, and even our nation's.

We will need to believe in a perspective and a higher purpose that includes not only our families and those close to us but all of humanity and all living things. We will need to recognize these intrinsic rewards as our path to joy and to saving our planet and ourselves.

PUTTING THIS BOOK IN PERSPECTIVE

Why am I writing about happiness? As much as this seems nice, how is it relevant to the workplace and group-level evolution?

Think about the good person/bad person lists you made. How are they different?

Every trait on the good person list is something that benefits that person's group. Generosity, kindness, humility, selflessness, forgiveness … etc. Objectively, these traits may or may not be good for the person exhibiting them. It is, however, unquestionably good for the group.

I am willing to bet that everything on your bad person list is something bad for that person's group. Selfishness, ego, anger, jealousy, and resentment, to name a few. Consider the so-called seven deadly sins: pride, greed, wrath, envy, lust, gluttony, and sloth. They are not really so bad for the person exhibiting them in the moment, assuming they can get away with it. They are really bad for that person's group. They also sound to me very much like a portrait of a value-calculating, rational, self-interested homo economicus.

Let's look at this the other way around. Consider the eight pillars of joy: perspective, acceptance, humility, humor, forgiveness, compassion, gratitude, and generosity. Try to imagine a human group surviving for any significant length of time without any one of these. Imagine a group with no compassion. A group with no generosity. How about a humorless group? If the group without compassion does not actually cease to exist, it will certainly be an underperforming and dysfunctional group.

These are not just "nice to have" individual qualities. They are essential for human groups and, because we are creatures who depend on our groups for survival, they are essential for *our* survival. That is why our brains are designed to reward us not so much for the behaviors that help us as individuals, but for those that help our groups. Fulfilling lives and sustained happiness come from doing the things that make our groups work well.

The only reason that work groups lacking these critical characteristics don't fail catastrophically is that we live in a relatively safe society, with friends and support systems outside our work lives.

In the 100,000 years of our evolution, where we evolved to be collaborative on the African plains or some primordial forest, we had only our family tribal group to ensure our survival. The groups who did not collaborate failed. We are the descendants of the collaborative groups. This is why we carry collaborative behavioral inclinations. This is why our brains reward us with bursts of oxytocin when we do something good for our group and even when we see someone else being compassionate and generous. Positive emotion, engagement, friendships, humility, humor, forgiveness, compassion, generosity, and gratitude are behavioral signs of a healthy and most likely successful human group.

One more word on perspective. Our beliefs about ourselves, the world, our company, and the other important humans in our environment are something we can control … somewhat. How we feel and, therefore, how we behave is largely dependent on what we believe. We are group creatures, however, and we are therefore shaped by the beliefs of others in our environment.

We need to choose the people in our environment carefully. Our beliefs need to be accurate. If we are working within an organization where selfish behavior is the norm, it will be unsafe to be altruistic. We will need to behave accordingly or leave. If we are a leader, we can consciously work to change it.

CHAPTER 6

Individual Uniqueness (We can't help it!) and Group Level Selection

You might think there is a tension between groups and individuals. If I want something for myself, isn't it likely to take away from the group? Having read this so far, you may be able to see that there is no such tension here. What do I truly deeply want? Happiness. What is the best way to be sustainably happy? Take care of my group. My authentic happiness and sustained fulfillment lie in doing the things I do well in service of my group and its purpose.

Some people will be thinking this sounds very warm and fuzzy. Very peace, love, and granola. That's just not real.

I challenge that view of reality. The business and workplace reality many of us believe in is a fiction that we created while we were in the nightmare homo economicus dream space. We created that fiction before we knew of the objective reality of how humans have been designed by evolution to want to make a contribution. The sooner we see this nightmare fictional reality created by economists and business schools preaching neoliberal economics for what it clearly is, the sooner we can move to a more real and more productive reality.

Conscious business is not just a nice idea. It is objectively "true," unlike the neoliberal homo economicus-based worldview, which is objectively untrue. Remember, homo economicus does not really exist; it is a fictional construction. Treating humans at work as if they are a homo economicus is a recipe for disaster, for the humans and for the business.

Humans are real and you can count on us to perform amazing things when we get the conditions right. As a Conscious Leader, it is your job to get those conditions right.

Here is a four minute video by John Mackey, co-founder of Whole Foods Market and the non-profit Conscious Capitalism, talking about Conscious Leadership. The Conscious Leader's job is to get the conditions for optimal human performance and happiness right. You might be surprised by what he boldly states in this short video.

There is a lot more to learn about us as individuals. If you have not read the latest research, prepare to be amazed.

Remember that fifty percent of our happiness is genetic? We all have a happiness range we tend to go back to. Some of us are more like glum Eyeore and some more like irrepressible Tigger. We just can't help it. If you are one of the lucky ones to win the genetic lottery and get a full dose of genetic Tiggerish happiness, congratulations! Would it be best for the group if everyone in the group were Tiggerish?

Happiness is not the only thing about our personalities that is genetically heritable. After many studies of identical and fraternal twins and other children raised in their natural families and those who were adopted at birth, the conclusion is that all personality traits are highly heritable, including being introverted or extroverted; optimistic or pessimistic; risk-taking or risk averse; liberal, conservative, or libertarian. We mostly can't help it. Okay, that's interesting, but why is it important?

First of all, we need to treat each other with a lot more understanding and patience. Obviously, I should not treat someone differently just because of their skin color. Skin color is just something they inherited genetically as did I, and it is not representative of them or me as a person. If to a large extent I can't help my personality traits, you should also be patient with me if you have a different point of view, and I should be patient with you. We should all patiently try to understand each other.

Why do we have these different personalities? Because we need mental diversity in our groups. It creates optimal performance! This is actually evolutionarily logical when we stop to think about it.

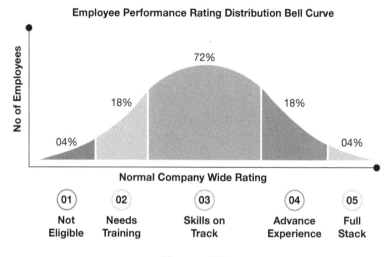

[Source: ???]

Does this HR bell curve show individual performance? Or does it show how well an organization is engaging people's skills and abilities? Some people (on the far right of the graph) seem to be highly engaged and able to make positive contributions that the organization values. Some (on the far left of the graph) are less engaged and not able to make contributions that the organization is valuing.

A company is like a boat. Some people are rowing hard, some are hardly rowing, and some are drilling holes in the boat, some of those holes are below the waterline.

What if the problem is not the people? What if the problem is organizational rigidity? What if we could move everyone up the scale? What if the people who were performing poorly and are most disengaged (the ones drilling holes in the boat) actually have the most impactful viewpoint we can learn from?

If you, your child, or best friend were graded a one or a two, how would you feel about the validity of this graph?

What this graph is really showing is the level of mismatch between people and the organization they are working in. Put that troublesome person in a different group or in a different company and they could be a superstar. Is that about selecting the right person for the job as most businesspeople see it? Putting the right people in the right seats in the bus? Or is it about building a different sort of bus? Creating a system in which jobs are highly flexible so that everyone (not just a lucky few) can engage and contribute in the way they do best. Remember, it is not just about the missing potential in the actively disengaged. It is also about the missing potential from the sleepwalking zombies, the people in the middle of the chart who are neither engaged nor actively disengaged. A huge potential improvement for the company if they become actively engaged. If most companies are doing a lot of work to find the right person to fit the job, why are there so many zombies wandering around and so many holes being drilled in our workplaces? Think about the time and effort in creating policies and job descriptions, compensation packages, and org charts. The time doing the screening processes, interviews, and evaluations. Add that to annual reviews, and it is a serious time suck and drag on the organization.

What if the problem is not in the people but in the organization? For one thing it would be a lot easier to fix. "Fixing" people is nearly impossible. Fixing an organization (though perhaps not a piece of cake) is a lot easier. What this graph shows is a huge opportunity for improvement if only we can get our organizational structure or operating system right.

Are you wondering where I got these ideas on genetics determining fifty percent of our personality? It came from this book, *Blueprint* by Robert Plomin.

BOOK REFLECTION

Blueprint: How DNA Makes Us Who We Are by Robert Plomin (2018)

Plomin is a genetic psychologist. He studies the effect of our genes on who we are.

We all share ninety-nine percent of our genes with each other. That's what makes us human. We share about ninety-seven percent of our genes with chimpanzees. It would not surprise you then to know that most of the ninety-nine percent of the genes we share make us mammals, give us two arms and two legs, give us a digestive system, etc.

The one percent of genes responsible for all our human variation controls things like eye color and height. That is easy to understand. If you or someone you know has struggled with body weight, you will not be surprised to learn that our genes also control things like our BMI, or body mass index. Yes, diet and exercise count, but seventy percent of our BMI is accurately predicted by our genes. BMI is highly heritable.

What might surprise you is the extent to which our genes are responsible for our personality.

Our personality is highly heritable. About fifty percent of our personality is encoded in our genes. Plomin studied identical twins adopted at birth and raised apart and found that they are remarkably similar. Children who are adopted show almost no correlation of BMI with their adoptive families but a lot of correlation to their birth parents, who they only knew for a few days.

There are literally thousands of genes that give us our personality, and many of these genes control other aspects of ourselves also.

There is another compounding aspect to this: the nature of nurture. If there are two children in a family, they will each get a share of their parents' DNA. Therefore, they will be different in size, shape, and personality, but also alike in some ways.

You can easily have one child who likes to read and one who does not in the same family. The one who enjoys reading may have been read to more when they were little. Did the parents treat them differently on purpose? Not at all. What happened is that one child asked to be read to and the other found it boring and did not. The parents were actually modified by their children more than the other way around. (Like the humorous bumper sticker that reads "Insanity is inherited; you get it from your children.") If one child is genetically antisocial, the parents may treat them more harshly. In this case it is not the harsh treatment that made the child antisocial, it is the other way around. If a child craves affection, their parents will spend more time cuddling them.

As we go out into the world, a lot of random stuff happens to us, and there is nothing we can do to control that. However, there are a lot of things under our control. Who chooses our friends? We do! Our choice in friends reinforces who we are.

Some people who read this may find it upsetting because after all, getting dealt a genetic hand not only on our gender, skin color, height, and weight but also our personality may seem a bit unfair and deterministic.

It does seem unfair that so much that contributes to our outcomes in life is determined genetically at conception. Then we tend to choose the things in life that reinforce our personality differences. The remainder of what influences us (socioeconomic status and the society into which we were born) is mostly random stuff that we have no control over. Genetic inequality is added to the inequality of our circumstances in which we grow up.

Here is my take on it though:

It feels unfair only because we are looking at it through a narrow lens of individual success, individual selection in a game of survival of the fittest individual. But what if life is about group level selection? What if we do well because our group does well?

Take Olympic sports as an example. Obviously success in pole vaulting requires a particular body type. Gymnastics is better suited to a person who is a bit smaller. Both athletes need to have little fear of heights though. The Olympics, like life, are not just one sport. We have been dealt a genetic hand and we have little control over the environment in which we grow up. But life is complex. Who is to say at the moment of our conception which hand will be best?

We are group creatures. Our individual success depends on the success of our group, and our group's success, in our unpredictable world, depends on having a wide variety of sizes, shapes, and personality types in it. Homogeneity is not helpful in group-level selection; individuality is. The only limiting factor in how varied our group can be is our need to get along and collaborate. A leader and the group's traditional norms determine the extent to which we either hold the space open for and celebrate differences, or not. As long as good collaboration can be maintained, the more diverse, open, and accepting a group is, the more successful it is likely to be.

It is not so important what traits I have been dealt. What is important is that our group can collaborate well with different individuals and make the best use of our differences to help the group.

If you can find a group that is highly accepting of differences and highly collaborative, where you feel you can openly bring your whole uniquely quirky self to work, you have probably found a group that is and will be successful.

Groups that are overly concerned and rigid about procedure, dress code, and job descriptions will not do as well.

I heard a talk by a young woman who had just earned her master's degree in business and was hired by a large company that wanted to increase their diversity. She had a very different ethnic and experiential background, she really needed the job, and she had school loans to pay off. She hated her job! She was required to comply with the strict dress code and do her work in the same precisely defined way as everyone else. She thought, "Why did they hire me? They could have hired anyone to do this job!"

What I would really like you to take away from this is that each of us is unique. I can't help being who I am, and you can't either. Neither can that young person you just hired. Work with the grain of human personality not against it. A company's success comes from respect and collaboration. Instead of trying to control people with rigid job descriptions, encourage job crafting. Let everyone's individual strengths come to bear on what we sense needs to be done at this moment in furtherance of our group's mission.

Instead of HR creating job descriptions, what if people doing the work created their job descriptions themselves? What if these descriptions were ever evolving as the group and external circumstances change?

If you are not familiar with Job Crafting here is a YouTube talk explaining the idea.

CHAPTER 7

Why Conscious Altruism in Business is True

> *"A bad leader is reviled by his people, a good leader is revered by his people. A great leader's people say We did it ourselves!"*
>
> —Lao Tzu

Now we are ready to dig into why conscious business is true. Unlike neoliberal economics, which was based on nothing objective at all, conscious capitalism's four principles are based on objective reality. The four principles of Conscious Capitalism are: Conscious Culture, Higher Purpose, Stakeholder Orientation, and Conscious Leadership. This may not be the order you are used to seeing them in, but for my purposes it makes more sense this way. All four principles are inextricably entwined. They are aspects of the same thing. It is not possible to talk about one without talking about the others. It's a system like a ball of yarn. You can start anywhere and follow it everywhere.

Hopefully, with the background we have already covered, the four principles will be more than just warm and fuzzy peace, love, and granola sentiments. They should make a lot of sense because we have an objective foundation on which they are built.

To see how these group behavioral systems can play out, what better way to run a natural experiment than to explore the history of shipwrecks on deserted islands!

BOOK REFLECTION

Blueprint: The Evolutionary Origins of a Good Society by Nicholas A. Christakis (2019)

Science and Shipwrecks!

(If you have been reading these book reflections, you may be experiencing a bit of deja vu. A previous reflection was also titled *Blueprint*, but it was by Robert Plomin.)

Plomin's book is about how each individual's set of genes is responsible for their unique personality. Anyone who has kids, or who has observed kids raised by the same parents in the same household knows this; each kid is different.

Christakis' book, on the other hand, is about how we behave in groups and what group behaviors work best. Christakis is a sociologist at Yale and writes about how our genetic coding ensures the ways in which we tend toward social sameness. His argument is that our evolutionary success came about because we were predisposed to express particular qualities and behaviors in groups.

This resonates because, as you may have heard me say before, we are group creatures. Our success depends on our group more than we

---

sometimes care to admit. It has been this way for hundreds of thousands of years, and it is probably even more true today than it was 50,000 years ago. We are not likely to survive long on our own, but as a group we do remarkably well.

Our individual differences in skills and abilities are essential for our group's survival. At the same time, our survival and the group's survival depend on the cohesiveness of the group. There is no tension between individuals growing in skill and self-knowledge and the group's success; it is one and the same thing, inextricably tied.

Christakis is focused on the things that keep us together. In this book he calls it "The Social Suite." At the core of all societies are eight critical things:

1. The ability to have and recognize individual identity
2. Love for partners and offspring
3. Friendship
4. Social networks
5. Cooperation
6. In-group preference
7. Mild hierarchy (that is, relative egalitarianism)
8. Social learning and teaching

Early in the book, Christakis illustrates the importance of these things. We can't test his hypothesis by setting up a control group in a social setting. However, sometimes natural experiments occur, and we can study those.

Christakis compares instances of groups of people who have been shipwrecked. Some groups did remarkably well, even under very adverse circumstances. All or nearly all of the people survived and were eventually rescued, sometimes several years after being shipwrecked. They did so, Christakis argues, because they modeled the social suite for optimal group performance. Other groups in arguably better circumstances, some of whom were shipwrecked on the same island at nearly the same time (almost a perfectly controlled experiment), had very few or no survivors because they did not embody these essential principles.

Just musing on some items in the social suite above will probably make it sort of obvious. Groups with authoritarian leaders who were not concerned about the lowest ranked members in the group did much more poorly than those with more egalitarian leadership. Bonds of friendship and social learning were also important. The more skills and abilities everyone has, the better off the group will be.

Christakis argues that this is the only successful strategy there is, with success equated to survival. We must embody these things if we are going to survive as a group.

If you were going to be shipwrecked tomorrow, would you choose to be shipwrecked with the other people in your company operating as your company currently does? If not, there is work to be done.

Admittedly, this is pretty strong stuff! And of course, in our daily lives we are not in such dire circumstances as a shipwreck (hopefully)! Therefore, we can sometimes get away with poor performance.

Without the social suite, our company may survive, but our performance will be miserable. And we will feel miserable. Does the following feel familiar?

Autocratic, self-centered people in leadership positions, people reluctant to share what they know for fear that the organization will no longer need them and leave them behind, lack of compassion and friendship at work, lack of trust in, and care for the group, fear of getting cut from the payroll when the chips are down … sound like a workplace you know of?

Think about it—there is no better example of the "chips are down" than being shipwrecked! Some groups took care of everyone, even the very sick and injured who were unlikely to ever be much help. These groups consistently did far better. Groups that left the sick and injured behind failed catastrophically, even when their circumstances were in many ways better. (This is akin to employees being cut because a business did not make a budget.)

Some businesses deliberately employ this toxic culture. Jack Welch was famous for his rank and yank policies. Rank everyone in the company and fire the bottom 10% every year. GE was once a great company known for innovation. By the time Welch left, it was a heartless husk of its former self. Little or no innovation, surviving by rigging the numbers of its financial products.

Just because we are lucky enough not to be shipwrecked does not mean that we should not be doing everything we can to improve our groups.

When I compare Christakis's social suite with the prosocial core design principles, I see the same theme emerging. And wouldn't you want these things in your shipwrecked group?

Prosocial Core Design Principles (David Sloan Wilson and Elinor Ostrom):

Strong group identity and understanding of purpose
Fair distribution of costs and benefits
Fair and inclusive decision-making
Monitoring agreed-upon behaviors
Graduated sanctions for misbehavior
Fast and fair conflict resolution
Authority to self-govern
Appropriate relations with other groups

If you are a leader in your company, it is your job to make sure your group is "coalescing" around the social suite and the prosocial design principles. Or to put it another way, if you are engaged in the embodiment of these things, you are a Leader. That is what leadership is.

> I need to mention that Social Suite number six, "In-group preference," is good for that group's success but only as long as it does not come at the expense of the success of any larger group system that it is part of. The HR department can have an in group preference for the HR department as long as it does not come at the expense of the company as a whole. A company can have an in group preference for itself as long as it does not come at the expense of it's economic ecosystem. What is good for a sub group may be bad for the larger group of which it is a part. If that is the case, then it will ultimately be bad for the sub group as well.

CONSCIOUS CULTURE

What is it? Let's start with what we now know about people.

We are group creatures, this is the objective reality. Our genes determine a lot about us, not only basic physical attributes like having two eyes, four limbs, and all the other physical ways we are similar but also all the ways we appear different; our relative size, eye color, hair color, and skin color, etc.

In the same way, but hidden from view, our genes are determining how our brains are constructed. Just like every other species, nature determines a lot of our behavior through genetic coding. Our basic behavior is similar to that of other humans. We respond more or less to the same extrinsic and intrinsic motivators. We know that, to create human well-being and flourishing, we need to create an environment full of intrinsically rewarding activity. We know that, for activities to be intrinsically rewarding, we need autonomy. We also know that environments in which humans have a great deal of autonomy and feel fulfilled give rise to the most high-performing human systems. Therefore, there is no tension between human well-being and flourishing teams of individuals and optimal group performance. It's different aspects of the same thing.

The first thing we need in a Conscious Culture then is <u>auton-omy</u> (or in Teal Organization terms, Self Management). Secondly, we need to provide as much opportunity for <u>intrinsically satisfying work and environment</u> as possible–things like learning, teaching, positive emotion, engagement, friendship, meaning, achievement, humility, humor, forgiveness, compassion, generosity, and gratitude.

We need to be able to <u>bring our whole selves to work</u>. For maximum performance, our companies also need us to bring our whole selves and perspectives into work every day.

Our <u>unique personalities</u> are encoded by our genes. Fifty percent of our personality is genetic. This personality predisposition leads to choices that reinforce this over time. The result is that, as we get older and have more life experience, we turn out even more like the person our genes predict we will be.

In a system where selection happens at the level of the group, it is beneficial to have a variety of individuals. This goes not only for physical characteristics but personalities as well. We evolved over hundreds of thousands of years living in the wild. To survive, it helped to have people who were very strong. But strength comes with a penalty. Strength requires muscle and having a lot of muscle requires a lot of food to maintain and can slow you down. Therefore, having some smaller, faster people is also useful. Variety is good. The same thing applies to individual personalities in our groups. I could be really good at one thing but terrible at something that you are very good at. As a team, we are stronger because we are different. The same applies to everyone in the group; the more variety the better.

This applies to personalities, too. Personality shapes how we view the world. Optimists are great because they see opportunity everywhere, but we also need pessimists to point out the flaws in an overly optimistic plan so that we can make a better plan. Without optimists, we might never spot opportunities staring us in the face. Without pessimists, we might make avoidable mistakes.

Objectively, we need a Conscious Culture that not only allows for a variety of personalities but actually encourages their expression.

So far, we have autonomy, intrinsic motivation, and a variety of personalities as parts of a conscious culture. What else do we need?

How about an operating system we can implement that encourages all this? As noted earlier Elinor Ostrom won the Nobel Prize in Economics for her CDP's (core design principles). She studied groups who collaborated to protect and care for their resources and did so successfully. Near the end of her life, she collaborated with evolutionary biologist David Sloan Wilson and they created the ProSocial Core Design Principles. These are the essential principles around which a successful high-performing human group is built.

- Strong group identity and understanding of purpose
- Fair distribution of costs and benefits
- Fair and inclusive decision-making
- Monitoring agreed-upon behaviors
- Graduated sanctions for misbehavior
- Fast and fair conflict resolution
- Authority to self-govern (individual autonomy)
- Appropriate relations with other groups (autonomy at the group level)

IMPLEMENTING A CONSCIOUS CULTURE

Recall that human behavior (culture) is generally driven by beliefs, which lead to emotions, that lead to behavior. Our emotional reactions and behavior are based on our self-view and worldview. (Our brains are prediction machines, and my emotions and behavior are based on the predictions my brain is making based on the beliefs I hold.) What do I believe about myself and what do I believe about my group? To implement a culture change, I need to change these two beliefs in a lot of people.

Fortunately we are very tuned into each other, so once we create a significant shift in a small number, most of the rest will follow. How do I change beliefs about people's selves and about the group? By offering information and examples of behavior that are contrary to people's beliefs but that are not too emotionally charged and at a rate they can handle.

What will not work is trying to make the same small change a step at a time throughout the whole organization.

What will work is creating a lot of change in a few small areas of the organization that are already favorably predisposed to the beliefs about themselves and the company that will lead to the behavior that you wish to encourage. Once this starts to grow, the rest will follow. (You will need some patience with some of the other groups.)

Lets get practical, *"Take chances, make mistakes, and get messy!"* said Ms. Frizzle (of *The Magic School Bus* television series). You can't steer a parked car. Don't overthink it; just get going. People are a complex system. Complex systems can't be completely comprehended or logically controlled. Therefore, we need to do what evolution does and experiment. The more experiments the better. Evolution works by variation, selection, and replication of what works. We can do the same.

One of the first mistakes most companies make is to try to plan it all out. This is a waste of time and detrimental to the process. Human systems are complex.

A word on the side about complex systems. Weather is a level one complex system. It is predictable to some extent for the next few days or so. We also know it will operate within a given range. (So far no 300 mph hurricanes or 200 degree days.) Humans are a level two complex system. A hurricane does not know that weather forecasters are making forecasts about it, and it does not change because of the forecasts. Humans, on the other hand, are aware that people are talking about them, attempting to influence them, and making predictions about them. So humans react to the environment and also to the influencers and predictions and may act in an unexpected way.

> *What is crucial is the relationship created between two or more elements. Systems influence individuals, and individuals call forth systems. It is the relationship that evokes the present reality. Which potential becomes real depends on the people, the events, and the moment. Prediction and replication are therefore impossible. While this is no doubt unsettling, it certainly makes for a more interesting world. People stop being predictable and become surprising. Each of us is a different person in different places. This does not make us inauthentic; it merely makes us quantum. Not only are we fuzzy; the whole universe is.*
>
> —Margaret Wheatley, *Leadership and the New Science*

Humans perceive reality, including subjective reality (Remember subjective reality? The beliefs we have and share?), changing around them and react in interesting, sometimes unexpected ways. We are reacting not only to changes in our own subjective reality; we are reacting to changes in others' subjective reality about a few things in particular: us personally (we are obsessed by what others think about us because it was evolutionarily important for our survival), our group, our larger group/company, and the subjective world we are operating in. This makes for a very complex system.

Just like the weather, though, we operate within bounded parameters. There are no 300 mph hurricanes and no 200-degree Fahrenheit days on earth. This is because of what in chaos theory is called a Lorenz attractor. Weather is unpredictable two months from now, but we can be quite certain that whatever is going on, it will be within definable boundaries. When building a weather prediction formula, the Lorenz attractor is a bit of "code" that keeps the predictions within boundaries. It is chaos within constraints. Predictably unpredictable within parameters.

The same thing applies to us. What we will be doing (or what the stock market will be doing) several days or months from now is not predictable, it is too complex. However, we are knowable.

What is our Lorenz attractor? What aspects of ourselves can we count on to be predictable?

Our built-in desire to do the things that give us intrinsic rewards is the Lorenz attractor in a human system. Evolution designed us to succeed as a group. These are the things we have been designed to desperately want: fairness, positive emotion, friendship, engagement, meaning, achievement, learning, teaching, humility, humor, compassion, generosity, gratitude, mild hierarchy, flexible leadership, group identity, purpose, and the freedom to just be ourselves.

For more completeness, I am also going to add to this list spirituality and a sense of oneness with the universe. This is not true for everyone, but it is something that many of us want. I think it is a component worthy of acknowledging.

These are the Lorenz attractors of a human system. When we have them in abundance, our groups are high-performing systems. When our groups are lacking in these things, we are a crippled group. For these attractors to have a positive effect on us, we must have autonomy. There can be no intrinsic reward without autonomy. If I force you or extrinsically incentivise you to do something, even a thing you would normally love doing, it will not be as satisfying as if you did it of your own volition. This is why commissioned artwork that is overly specific is not intrinsically satisfying to the artist and will not be of the inspiring high quality the artist typically produces.

We naturally want these intrinsic motivators and are designed for them, so why don't our groups always have them? Unfortunately, as in the case of shareholder capitalism, the subjective realities we sometimes create about business run counter to optimal human design principles for both people and their organizations.

Here is a video of Gary Hamel, professor at the London Business School, talking about the gifts of initiative, imagination, and passion.

KIDS AND CRAYONS

BOOK REFLECTION

***Punished by Rewards: The Trouble with Gold Stars, Incentive Plans, A's Praise, and Other Bribes* by Alfie Kohn (1993)**

This book has been around for twenty-five years, challenging the old "carrot and stick" philosophy of how to motivate people. It's still one of my favorites, and in my opinion deserves a read and a place on every manager's shelf. For perspective, though, I'll start with W. Edwards Deming, founder of Total Quality Management (TQM). You've probably heard of him.

"One is born with intrinsic motivation, self-esteem, dignity, cooperation, curiosity, joy in learning. These attributes are high at the beginning of life, but are gradually crushed by the forces of destruction."

"The forces of destruction come from the present style of reward, and their effects. What they do is to squeeze out from an individual, over his lifetime, his innate intrinsic motivation, self-esteem, dignity. They build into him fear, self-defense, extrinsic motivation. We have been destroying our people, from toddlers on through university, and on the job. We must preserve the power of intrinsic motivation, dignity, cooperation, curiosity, joy in learning that people are born with."

—*W. Edwards Deming, The New Economics*

As management legend goes, Deming's advice on manufacturing quality was falling on deaf ears here in the U.S., but he found a rapt audience when he took his ideas to Japan after WWII. He is probably the key person responsible for the quality turnaround in Japanese products. This was most evident in the auto industry. U.S. automobile quality was terrible, Japan was worse, but they listened, and Toyota quickly became and is still a dominant car maker in the U.S. Honda, Subaru, Nissan, and others are also doing quite well.

What you may not expect from such a guru on manufacturing quality and performance is something like his quote above. Deming comes out very clearly and firmly against extrinsic reward systems!

Here is another Deming quote to reinforce that point:

"The idea of a merit rating is alluring. The sound of the words captivates the imagination: 'pay for what you get; get what you pay for; motivate people to do their best, for their own good.' Well, the effect is exactly the opposite of what those words promise. Everyone propels himself forward, or tries to, for his own good, on his own life preserver. The organization is the loser" (Deming 1986).

Alfie Kohn's (1999) book, *Punished by Rewards*, is all about this. This is one of my favorite examples of how rewards backfire, pulled from its pages.

A group of psychological researchers is studying the effect of different sorts of rewards. The study is done using young children in a school setting and starts with the researchers handing out art supplies. It is a free period, so the children can do whatever they like. As you might expect, some kids chase eachother around the room, but a great number of them settle down to make some art. The researchers take note of which kids are engaged in artwork. With this baseline established, the next week begins the experiment.

The following week, kids who spent the most time doing artwork are randomly divided into three groups. The first is the control group. They are given the art supplies and just like the first week, they settle down to do art. The second group is a test group. They are told that if they do great artwork today they will be given an art appreciation award. This award is a ribbon of the sort schools often give out (I am sure you have seen them). This group settles down and does art just like the first group and just like they did the first week. At the end of the period, each child in the second group is given an art appreciation award as they have been promised. The third group is also given art supplies and they settle down to do art. At the end of the time, they are all surprised by being given an art appreciation award. They were not expecting it!

The third week rolls around and again the control group is given art supplies and they settle down and do art. The second group is given art supplies and told that unfortunately, "We are all out of art appreciation awards." This second group proceeds to do almost no art. The third group is given the art supplies and told that unfortunately, "We are all out of art appreciation awards." This group settles down and does the same amount of art as the first group.

What happened to the second group? They liked to do art. They were randomly selected from kids who liked to do art. The third group did not get any rewards either and were told that there were none, but they did just as much art anyway.

The difference is subtle but obviously extremely important. The kids in the second group were given an if/then reward. If you do this, then you will get that. The third group was given a "now this!" reward. They were not expecting anything, and yet they got a reward.

The second group was doing something they liked doing. However, while they were doing it, they were thinking about an extrinsic reward. And it was a really small thing, just a ribbon.

An if/then reward is an extrinsic reward. It is essentially, as the title of the book suggests, a bribe. The kids were all randomly selected from a group of kids who intrinsically liked to do art. They quickly became trained not to do a thing they enjoyed unless there was something extra in it for them. They were refocused on the extrinsic reward instead of the art itself. As Deming says so well, "squeezing out their innate intrinsic motivation."

The third group was unaffected because they did not expect the reward, hence it did not become a bribe. They were still doing the art because they just liked doing it. The presence of a reward or lack thereof the third week was therefore of no negative consequence.

One of the great joys in life is doing what we do well for the benefit of our group.

When our workplace gives us bribes to do what we do best and what we love doing, it squeezes out the intrinsically rewarding nature of our work life. If this continues to happen, as Deming says, it will also destroy our motivation, self-esteem, and eventually our dignity. Who wants to do that to anyone? Extrinsic rewards turn high performers into low performers, and the company is the looser.

How many of our workplace systems are set up to extrinsically motivate us?

Now I know that some people may read this and think, *But I can't get people motivated any other way!* If that's true, and to some extent I hear you and agree with you, it is not because people are born to be extrinsically motivated. It is rather because they were trained to become that way, through reinforcement over time. Effectively, many managers have unwittingly "destroyed" the altruistic impulse their people were born with! The destruction may not have occurred during a person's time in your company. It may have begun at school, as Deming suggests, and continued at other places they have worked previously. It will take some time and patience to reset.

Knowing this, we need to reset work practices. Eliminate all extrinsic rewards (bribes) from the workplace. Including even (and this might come as a shock!) the bribes considered essential to motivate that separate species of human, the "salesperson" who is usually the primary target of these bonuses/bribes. You want your sales people thinking about the customer's needs and how your company can creatively help them, not how large their bonus is going to be. So, compensate them fairly, with an amount typical for a salesperson living where they are and doing the work they do in your type of industry. I would also suggest you pay above average. The salary should be enough to take the issue of money and fixation on bonuses and other bribes off the table and out of mind. This includes stock options which as is often claimed have not been shown to create an owner's mentality. Your salespeople and other staff can now focus on doing what they love to do: find that sweet spot where the company provides what the customer needs.

If/then rewards are particularly destructive. "Now this!" rewards (the kind the third group of kids were given) can become "if/then" rewards if they become expected. If every time you do something I surprise you with a gift card, you will begin to expect a gift card when you do it. It has now become an if/then reward. If you do the thing and you don't get a gift card, you might even ask me why I didn't give it to you.

Don't let HR tell you (as my HR department did) that we need to set up a gift card reward system to reward ABC-type behaviors predictably and equally with XYZ rewards and that all managers should have a meeting and agree on the metrics we would all use consistently to give them out. That's the surest path to an if/then reward system. Treating people fairly is not the same as treating them equally. We want to be treating people fairly. Fairly means treated as the individual (i.e, distinctly different) person I am. Conformity does not equal fairness.

Now, I do like surprising people with gift cards. Or just seeking out someone to thank for a job well done. It's fun! Just keep mixing it up.

People should be coming to work for the intrinsic rewards. Two Intrinsic rewards are positive emotion and relationships. So, a high-five is a good thing. Someone may be a consistent high performer and not get a lot of recognition, yet they are happily engaged in what they find fulfilling every day. Work can be (and should be) its own reward. Someone else who has been working really hard to learn a new job may just barely manage something for the first time. It might be far from perfectly executed, and it may have taken the person a lot of time to do it, but they did it! High-five!

So am I saying eliminate all extrinsic rewards: bonus money, special parking places, a corner office, a company car, etc?

If it is an if/then bribe to elicit a certain behavior then yes, that is exactly what I am saying. If it is rare, spontaneous, and unexpected, a fairness issue or a group reward, then it is okay.

If, for example, everyone who works for the company for twenty years gets XYZ, then you can keep doing that. That is just a fairness thing. It is not something you did as an individual to get it; it is something related to the job or role you are doing and everyone who is in that same group doing that same thing gets the identical thing, no more or less. That's just fairness. Fairness is good.

It is also better to give rewards to groups instead of individuals. That fosters group collaborative effort instead of selfish effort. We don't want to create a system in which an individual wins and "the organization is the loser" as Deming says. Don't encourage self-interest over group interest.

The best sort of reward is a bonus (pizza for everyone on Friday, or a company trip, or whatever) to everyone in the company. After all, everyone who showed up contributed to the company's success that week. It is best to give the same amount to everyone, regardless of position, or possibly even more to those who earn less. It will mean more to them, and we all like taking care of each other. Leaders who take care of those who need it most are regarded much more favorably by their group. If you want to instill loyalty, take care of the ones who need the most help. We all care about and will protect our group when our group cares about and protects the most vulnerable among us. We will all care about and protect our leaders when they are caring about and protecting those of us who are most vulnerable. It's a sign of healthy leadership and a healthy group.

In any case, sharing an if/then reward with everyone in the company, or possibly just the people in a given location, signals that we are a team, and we are all in this together, which is exactly the message we want to send. We may be thinking about this reward while we are doing our work, but we will be thinking of the good it will do for the others in our group. It is no longer a selfish motivation. Now I am motivated by doing something good for my whole group.

How powerful are intrinsic rewards? Compare the Russian army with Ukraine's. You have probably heard the commentators say that the Ukrainians are doing so well because they are defending their country and that is a powerful motivator.

The Russians are being extrinsically motivated by threats, punishments, or rewards. The Ukrainians are intrinsically motivated to protect their group. The Russians are willing to do only the bare minimum for the extrinsic motivators. The Ukrainians are willing to risk everything to protect each other.

What gets in the way of our intrinsically rewarding, high-performance, human system Lorenz attractors?

Virtually everything "normal" businesses do. Individual extrinsic if/then rewards. (Individual bonuses are just about always bad, even for that presumably different human subspecies we call salespeople.) Group bonuses are good if they are a result of an agreed upon group fairness principle. Profit sharing is a good example of a good if/then reward. If we attain profits of X amount, we will distribute Y to all of you fairly. That's just plain fair, remember the capuchin monkeys? Keep in mind, though, that profits are only an outcome of a business; they are not why the business exists.

Performance reviews, strategic plans, budgeting, job descriptions, organizational charts, job interviews, and many rules and procedures can all be detrimental to autonomy and intrinsic rewards and detrimental to high-performing human systems. This is true if (as they usually are) they are done for the wrong reasons or in the wrong way. Ask yourself why these are being done and what good is expected in the outcome.

Strategic plans, budgets, job descriptions, org charts, and interview processes—you may find that you need to redesign them or just eliminate them. Remember, they are all subjective reality, fictional stuff we made up. Your strategic plan, like your budget, is a fiction you created. I am not saying it is a bad thing to do. I am just saying remember it is a fiction, and when reality starts to unfold differently, we need to adjust our story or abandon it. Our world is complex, and it is not likely to conform to our expectations and plans much of the time. Holding people accountable for a fiction makes no sense. Planning is invaluable. Plans may be worthless.

If your strategic plan and budget are looking spot-on a month or so after you create them, you are probably not paying close enough attention to the changing world outside and inside your organization. It is only a worldview, a perspective about your company and the world. It is going to change. The same thing applies to org charts, job descriptions, and performance reviews. These are all fictions based on perspective. They are useful predictions that need to be continually updated. Do not let that get in the way of a clear view of unfolding, objective reality.

This is exactly the way your brain works. Remember your brain is a prediction organ. It predicts what is about to happen based on a self-view and worldview. The more you plan and predict, the less objective reality you may see. Your paradigm constrains your reality. What you perceive is mostly the world your brain made up before it happened. Your brain provides an emotion when there is a mismatch between your perspective and emerging objective reality. If that emerging objective reality is too contrary to your perspective, you may have an adverse emotional reaction and reject it altogether.

> "We have a strategic plan. It's called 'doing things.'"
> —Herb Kelleher, Co-founder of Southwest Airlines

Remember, we created and maintain this fictional reality. If it is serving us, we will be a company of engaged, flourishing human beings who are excited to come to work and leave exhausted but fulfilled, having done what we do best for our group, and all is good. If it is not serving us, and if it is in conflict with the objective reality of what we know of human beings, it needs to be changed.

We are good at designing realities. It is our super power. As with all super powers, it works best when we know we have it.

BOOK REFLECTION

71/2 Lessons about the Brain by Lisa Feldman Barrett (2020)

This is a very short, easily read book by one of the leading researchers in psychology and neuroscience. I read all 130 pages in one morning, and I am not a particularly fast reader.

My hope is that this reflection on the 71/2 lessons will inspire you to get a copy and read it.

Chapter/Lesson ½: "Our Brains Are Not for Thinking." Evolution gave us brains to manage the systems going on in our bodies (body budgets) and foster our efficient survival in the world. Our brains are prediction machines. Based on past experience and our view of "reality," our brains predict what will happen in our environment. Predictions are designed to keep us alive and to save energy resources. Our predictive brains find it annoying when I don't finish the ....

Chapter/Lesson 1: "We Have One Brain, Not Three." We don't have a lizard brain for survival, a mid-brain for emotions, and a logical brain to rule them all. We have just one brain. There is no tension between three fictitious ideas. Emotion and reason are not separate things.

Chapter/Lesson 2: "Our Brains Are Networks." Not every cell is connected to every other. That would create what Barrett calls a "meat-loaf brain," a homogeneous mass not capable of anything interesting. Our brains are also not like Swiss army knives; they are not a fixed set of tools pre-wired in a particular way that can do a few specific things. Our brains are networks. When we learn something new, a network is created. If we use it often, it is strengthened. If we don't use it, the connections fade away, a process of "tuning and pruning."

Chapter/Lesson 3: "Little Brains Wire Themselves to the World." Unlike most species, we develop late. The whole wiring process takes about twenty-five years. This allows our brains the flexibility needed to wire themselves for the environment and the society we are born into.

Chapter/Lesson 4: "Your Brain Predicts (almost) Everything You Do." This is one of the brain's main functions. Based on current circumstances and past experience, our brains are continually predicting our environment and planning our next moves, even executing the next moves before the sensory data of the "real world" is processed. Your brain is designed to initiate your actions before you are aware of them. Predicting and acting is almost always ahead of understanding. Fighter pilots talk of the OODA loop: Observe, Orient, Decide, Act. This is a misconception. It would take far too long, and you would end up dead. Our brains use a predict, begin to act, correct, predict again, begin modified action, correct again … continuous system. The only thing remotely like deciding is the prior experience our brains are drawing from to make the predictions. This is where we have agency (free will) over our behavior. We can decide what we learn and how we want to perceive the world and gradually train ourselves to see it that way. Is it a world of scarcity or of abundance? Both beliefs are true. If you believe in scarcity you are correct. If you believe in abundance you are also correct. Your belief creates your reality. Which belief are we going to choose to train ourselves to see more clearly? This is what the Dalai Lama (2016) calls "perspective" in *The Book of Joy* mentioned earlier.

Chapter/Lesson 5: "Your Brain Secretly Works with Other Brains." We are a group species. We need and affect each other more than we know. Ubuntu is the idea that we call each other into being, and this is very close to the mark. Solitary confinement is a slow form of capital punishment. We regulate each other's brains and "body budgets." Barrett writes, "Have you lost someone close to you through a breakup or a death and felt you had lost part of yourself? That's because you did. You lost a source of keeping your body systems in balance" (p86).

"The price of personal freedom is personal responsibility for your impact on others. The wiring of our brains guarantees it" (p96).

The freedom to say whatever we want comes with the responsibility of the effect our speech has on others. Because we are social creatures, we will all enjoy the fruits of uplifting speech and the suffering due to harmful speech.

Chapter/Lesson 6: "Brains Make More Than One Kind of Mind." We are not all the same. We have different personalities, and on top of that, our brains construct themselves differently when we are raised in a different society. This is why immersing ourselves in a different culture where we don't know the first thing about that society's norms (or language) is so difficult. What was automatic in our own society now must be learned again. Understanding each other is going to be more critical to the future survival of humanity. Abe Lincoln is alleged to have said, "I don't like that man. I must get to know him better."

Chapter/Lesson 7: "Our Brains Can Create Reality." Barrett writes, "Social reality can alter dramatically, in moments, if people simply change their minds. In 1776, for example, a collection of thirteen British colonies vanished and was replaced by the United States of America" (p111).

This is a super power that only we humans have. We can create money, towns and states, democracy, and human rights just by believing it is so. And just as easily, we can lose something valuable if we cease to believe in it. Barrett explains, "We have more control over reality than we might think. We have more responsibility for our reality than we might realize ... A superpower works best when you know you have it" (Barrett p123).

Want to have some fun and run an experiment? Next time you are involved in strategic planning use the 71/2 lessons as a framework. Afterall lesson ½ is our brains are prediction organs. Most of lessons 1–7 are how our brains do that.

Culture is not monolithic, and it shouldn't be.

Most company leaders will erroneously assume (and most consultants are guilty of this also) that they need to drive the whole organization toward one unified company culture and that this is necessary for it to be most productive. There are a great many business culture books on the market that would have you think so. They are wrong.

Do you remember the TV series M.A.S.H.? How effective would that M.A.S.H. unit have been if it conformed to military cultural norms? Yes, the 4077th was part of a larger military culture and, in its contacts with that larger system, it matched protocol appropriately. However, it had its own distinct culture and performed at a high level because of that culture. Their culture allowed individuals to be themselves. The characters who attempted to minimize the key cultural components of freedom of expression and individuality were gently chided, or in some cases, forced out.

There are two human principles that we need to keep in mind: autonomy and individuality.

The culture in your accounting department will be different from the culture in your marketing department. That's as it should be. They are doing different types of work. Accounting is mostly algorithmic work like following a recipe where rules are rules. You can't just put a number in a different column or change the font because it looks prettier that way. Marketing is mostly heuristic work requiring creativity where "rules" (if any) are just guidelines. These two professions also attract different personality types. One group will be more comfortable when there are clearly defined rules. The other group will chafe at rules. You will probably have noticed that computer programmers and preschool teachers have different personality types. The culture is different because the work is different and because these are different sorts of people. Don't fight it; cherish it.

Some of us desire uniformity and conformity, especially if it is conformity to what we perceive as normative and correct behavior. Some of us have this personality trait to a high degree. As a leader, your job is to allow such conformity (and comfort) within the group who desires it but allow variation in all other places.

Every group in your company can and should have its own culture. Your job as the leader is to make sure that's possible. You should see to it that everyone can bring their whole self to work. Likewise, each group should be able to operate in a culture that feels right and works for them. You are holding the space for variation and evolution. You will be challenged by the group that prefers uniformity. They will believe that everyone should have the same culture and that theirs is the right one. Your job is to encourage autonomy, individuality, variety, and experimentation. Just as you need to encourage people to bring their individual whole selves to work because that individuality is a strength for the organization, you also need to encourage groups to bring their whole selves to work. First shift may have a different personality than the third shift. That's awesome. Help them share who they are (which spreads good ideas) and, at the same time, encourage the individuality of the group. Not every good idea is good for everyone or every group.

We are not putting people on the right seat in the corporate bus. We are allowing people to create all sorts of transportation options for themselves and their groups. Whatever works best for them.

Variation, selection, and replication of what works is the evolutionary formula. This does not mean that we are driving toward a meatloaf of uniformity. What applies to our individual brains applies to our collective brains and groups. As Barrett says in lesson 2 of *71/2 Lessons About the Brain*, our brains are not meatloafs of uniformity. The same concept applies to our human groups; our groups should not be meatloafs. Not every cell or person should be like every other. Not every group of people should be the same as every other. Nor should we be like that fixed Swiss army knife of tools. We should be a network of abilities that is constantly undergoing a process of tuning and pruning. What we do a lot we get better at (tuning), and what we do seldomly gradually falls away. We are constantly evolving and maintaining a diversity of skills and abilities. Companies like little brains (lesson 3) are constantly wiring themselves to the world anew.

Just as individuals have personalities, groups have personalities. This is the fractal nature of humanity. A fractal thing looks the same at both a small scale and a larger scale. A small group of individuals, each with a different personality, looks just like a group of groups, each with its own personality. A large company also has a personality. When we view a group of companies together, an individual company's culture or personality comes into focus. We need the larger context to see cultural differences.

CONSCIOUS CULTURE

Conscious Culture is what we humans want and need to form a high-performance group. It has the following:

1. Autonomy (a prerequisite for intrinsic rewards)
2. An intrinsically rewarding work environment
3. Engagement (we want to do what we do best for our group)
4. Minimal hierarchy, egalitarian environment
5. Ability to bring our whole selves to work
6. Purpose

To operationalize this, remember Elinor Ostrom and David Sloan Wilson's Prosocial Core Design Principles:

- Strong group identity and understanding of purpose
- Fair distribution of costs and benefits

- Fair and inclusive decision-making
- Monitoring agreed-upon behaviors
- Graduated sanctions for misbehavior
- Fast and fair conflict resolution
- Authority to self-govern
- Appropriate relations with other groups

Look for the small part of your company that exemplifies or leans in this direction and start there. If you have found the right sort of place, people there will take to it like ducks to water. You want to do a lot in this small space before rolling it out to other parts of the organization. Ideally, many other areas of the organization will be a bit jealous of what this first, small group gets to do before you give others the green light. Eventually, nearly everyone will be eager to make the change.

Your job will be to remove obstacles for this first group. You will find that many of the things that helped your organization to its current level of success are now preventing it from going further.

Imagine a bell curve. At one end of the curve is a company that is struggling. It may not exist a few months from now. Some consultants are hired to "turn it around." They set up things like a board of directors, strategic plans, budgets, job descriptions, clear reporting structures, performance reviews, bonus structures, and organizational charts. There is a lot of talk of holding people accountable. If it all works out, the company gets on its feet. It is now benchmarked firmly under the middle of the bell curve. The consultants all congratulate themselves and go on to the next rescue mission.

But what about those companies at the far end of the bell curve? The ones that are doing incredibly well? The ones whose customers will not even consider going anywhere else? The ones whose employees can't be enticed away by larger salary and bonus offers? The ones whose shareholders are loyal and very pleased with their investment?

Most if not all of the things those consultants implemented to move that company to the middle of the bell curve are now keeping it from moving beyond the middle of the bell curve. It is your job to allow those constraints to be removed.

GROUP PURPOSE

"For success, like happiness, cannot be pursued; it must ensue, and it only does so as the unintended side-effect of one's personal dedication to a cause greater than oneself or as the by-product of one's surrender to a person other than oneself. Happiness must happen, and the same holds for success: you have to let it happen by not caring about it."

—Viktor E. Frankl, *Man's Search for Meaning*

"This is the true joy in life: being used for a purpose recognized by yourself as a mighty one. Being a force of nature instead of a feverish, selfish, little clod of ailments and grievances, complaining that the world will not devote itself to making you happy."

—George Bernard Shaw, *Man and Superman*

Purpose is a strong driver for each of us as individuals. We should all know our individual purpose in life and be making personal decisions based on that purpose. Humans are fractal creatures. As Lisa Feldman Barrett indicates, we are really a part of each other. When we lose a friend, we feel as though we have lost a part of ourselves because we actually have. Just as we have a personal purpose and we are intrinsically motivated by doing the things we do best for our group, our group operates best when it has a clear purpose and is feeling intrinsically motivated to do what it does best for some other group or cause beyond ours. This is group-level intrinsic motivation.

Articulating group purpose can come easily or take a lot of work. If all of the members of the group hold similar beliefs about "reality," if they share similar intersocial subjective reality and understand the world in a similar way, including a shared view of what they do well as a group and what the outside world needs, articulating its higher purpose will be easier. If the group diverges on its view of reality, what the group does well, and what the outside world needs, this will be more difficult.

Consultants are frequently hired to help with the process of discovering and articulating group purpose. What the consultants are being engaged to do is to unify and possibly change group behavior, which requires changing group beliefs about themselves and the world. As my psychology professor said, to change behavior at the level of the individual, you need to be a significant other, someone the person trusts, and then offer views that differ from their self-view and worldview but that are not too emotionally charged and at a rate they can handle.

Finding group purpose is the same process but at the level of the group. The consultant must be someone the group trusts and who can tease out the group's self-view and worldview for examination and assessment. Are these views serving the group? As the process unfolds, the group's self-view becomes more clear. Members may or may not consciously choose to change it. They now know who they are and what they do well. They know what motivates them as a group. They also become more clear on what the world needs and how they can make that happen in their unique way. This is group purpose.

Clearly held beliefs about ourselves, our group, and the world come first, and this leads naturally to an emotional response. If we have been clear about our beliefs, we will be intrinsically motivated as a group to do what we believe we do well, for some group or purpose beyond our group. (Intrinsic reward comes from doing some good, true, beautiful, and possibly even heroic thing for someone or something other than your group.) You know you have done a good job of finding purpose when the group believes that the purpose is worthy and emotionally compelling.

Why have a purpose? Three reasons. First, because it is a really strong human motivator. This can't be overstated; an engaging purpose is a huge performance driver. We humans are wired for this. Second, because it enhances autonomous decision making. Third, purpose is a key reason why people come to work engaged and ready to make a contribution. It fulfills us to be a key part of a group that is working toward a purpose greater than ourselves.

If I need to make a decision in an unusual circumstance, I can use our shared purpose to decide whether what I intend to do is aligned with our purpose or not. If it is aligned, then the decision is probably "Go." If it is not, then it's a "No-go." If the degree of alignment is unclear, then I should probably discuss it with others.

Hopefully you can see that purpose is an intersocial subjective reality. To reiterate, just because it is a subjective reality does not mean it is not real. Human rights are an intersocial subjective reality. They are "true" because we believe them to be. Purpose can be good, like the UN's (2015) sustainable development goals. They further human well-being globally.

Purpose can also be bad. Many wars and riots have occurred due to beliefs about reality that were actually false (inconsistent with objective reality, e.g., voter fraud in the 2020 U.S. election) or were at odds with a different group's subjective reality.

You can craft your company's purpose in several ways. As the leader, you can dictate it, you can let your management team dream it up, or you can reach out to the whole organization and synthesize it based on the feedback you get.

The best approach probably depends on the organization. If you are an early startup and you are the founder and you know why you started this, you can and possibly should just declare it. Everyone who joins will know what you are about and can join if your company's purpose aligns with their own.

If you are an established company that has never articulated or even discussed a purpose or values before, it could make sense to have the management team come up with it.

If, however, you have talked about purpose before, and your company has a clear sense of established if not articulated values that you are happy with, it might be a good time to reach out to literally everyone and see what they reflect back to you. If you have been sending a strong and consistent vibe, you will probably hear a resonant vibe back.

If you are a startup, it will not take long to disseminate the company purpose. If you are larger and you dictate it or you have the management team come up with it, you will have the additional task of disseminating it to everyone. This will take some time. If you invite the whole company to be involved, it will take more time initially to divine the purpose, but you will save a lot more time and effort later because everyone will already be thinking about it and be tuned in to the discussion. It will take root faster and deeper.

In our family business, the management team came up with a purpose for Watson, Inc. It explained who we were and why we existed. We said "We are an invested fellowship fostering health and happiness for all." Invested fellowship meant that we were invested in each other's personal growth. Our why for being was to foster health and happiness for all, both our company group and larger society. This fit well with our being a food company making nutritional products, vitamin and mineral products, and also some products that were just fun, such as edible glitter.

Is purpose fractal? Absolutely! The marketing team could have a sub-group purpose that aligns with and supports the overall company purpose. So could the IT department and manufacturing. I say _could_ because, at this level, it should not be a mandatory thing. I think the autonomy of the group is key, and therefore, I would let the group decide for itself if it should have its own stated purpose and if so what that is. The accounting group could do it, and if the collections department, which is under accounting, wants to do it, they should also. Ideally, every person in the company knows and can articulate what their personal purpose is. In one company I know, it's a requirement that each person state their personal purpose within three months of being hired. I think making it a requirement is going too far, but, that certainly makes stating a personal purpose a cultural norm and not an odd thing to do.

Do not underestimate the power of stating your purpose. Imagine an accounting department whose purpose is to provide the required financial information for compliance with tax code regulations, for bank loan agreements, and for the CEO and management team. That might sound fairly typical. Now imagine an accounting department whose purpose is to provide timely, actionable, easy-to-comprehend information to all individuals and departments to enhance their knowledge of the current state of the business and to support proactive, collaborative and autonomous decision-making in each department.

In the first case, everyone will end up being subjects of the accounting department, who will demand accountability to a budget. In the second case, the accounting department is in service to every other group in the organization. This is the difference between a somewhat selfish group purpose and a collaborative, altruistic group. In reality of course, the work done is going to be both. We can't ignore tax law. However, complying with tax law is merely table stakes. Purpose needs to be more than that, it needs to be inspiring.

If you are clear on your group purpose and you articulate it well, you will find and attract others on the same journey.

> "If you do follow your bliss you put yourself on a kind of track that has been there all the while, waiting for you, and the life that you ought to be living is the one you are living. When you can see that, you begin to meet people who are in your field of bliss, and they open doors to you. I say, follow your bliss and don't be afraid, and doors will open where you didn't know they were going to be."
>
> —Joseph Campbell and Bill Moyers, *The Power of Myth*

STAKEHOLDERS

As you may have gleaned earlier, I am a big fan of David Sloan Wilson's (2007) statement:

> "Selfishness beats altruism within groups. Altruistic groups beat selfish groups. All else is commentary."

One of the four principles of Conscious Capitalism is Stakeholder Orientation. Stakeholder Orientation is objectively true for human beings. The shareholder system is not objectively true for human beings.

The quote above explains why. When there is a selfish actor within a group containing altruistic individuals, the selfish individuals will take advantage of the altruistic individuals. This will lead to benefits for the selfish individuals but also to poor group performance. Altruistic groups outperform groups containing selfish individuals because they can create more for everyone.

A shareholder orientation on the other hand is the belief that a company exists solely for the benefit of the shareholders. This comes out of the neoliberal economic view that believes we humans are homo economici, which, if you've been following my arguments, is demonstrably untrue. We are not predominantly selfish. We are not coldly rational or even mostly rational. Survival of the fittest individual is a limited belief system propped up by some economists and capitalists, not simply "the way things are."

Evolution only cares about effective survival. As we have seen, evolution designed humans for group-level selection. Evolution did this not because she was feeling all warm and fuzzy that day, but because it works better! A group of collaborative individuals will outperform a group of selfish individuals. We see this again and again; it's a truth we can rely on. Variation, selection, and replication of what works, and it turns out that altruism works best. We only need to be vigilant about removing selfish behavior from the group to make it possible.

It is also fractal. It is as evident at the level of small groups as it is for big groups (or groups of groups). Logically, it follows that groups of companies collaborating altruistically will outperform groups of selfish companies competing against each other for their own personal gain. That's the objective (factual) reason why a stakeholder orientation outperforms a shareholder orientation. This is one reason why Conscious Companies outperform regular companies.

The shareholder version of capitalism is objectively incorrect. Ayn Rand was wrong. Neoliberal economics is wrong. It is a toxic and false intersocial subjective reality. When we believe in this falsehood and business schools teach it, it is easier to perpetuate the myth, easier for people to accept it, and easier to excuse selfish behavior. Do not accept it. This malevolent myth, if unchecked, leads to planetary destruction. I am not exaggerating. We need to stop excusing the behavior that this philosophy engenders by saying it is just business. It is not just business. It is objectively wrong.

The stakeholder principle applies at every level, from individuals in a small group to small groups within a company, and all the way to groups of companies collaborating with other companies and states collaborating with other states and nations with other nations, all the way to the highest levels of altruistic engagement. Locally and globally, altruistic groups outperform selfish groups.

> "And all I am saying is simply this, that all life is interrelated. Somehow we are tied to a single garment of destiny, caught in an inescapable network of mutuality, where what affects one directly affects all indirectly. As long as there is poverty in this world, you can never be totally rich, even if you have a billion dollars. As long as diseases are rampant and millions of people cannot expect to live more than thirty or thirty two years, you can never be totally healthy, even if you just got a clean bill of health from the Mayo Clinic or John Hopkins Hospital. Strangely enough I can never be what I ought to be until you are what you ought to be, and you can never be what you ought to be until I am what I ought to be. This is the way the world is made."
>
> —Rev. Martin Luther King, Jr. 1960

CONSCIOUS LEADERSHIP

> "If you create an environment where the people truly participate, you don't need control. They know what needs to be done and they do it. And the more that people will devote themselves to your cause on a voluntary basis, a willing basis, the fewer hierarchies and control mechanisms you need."
>
> —Herb Kelleher, in Jeffrey Krames' *What the Best CEOs Know*

"A bad leader is reviled by his people. A good leader is revered by his people. A great leader's people say 'We did it ourselves!'"
—Lao Tsu (AKA Laozi) 6th Century BCE

Why does Conscious Capitalism work so well?

- Because altruistic groups outperform selfish groups (Stakeholder Orientation)
- Because groups with clearly articulated shared beliefs in who they are and their mission in the world outperform groups who are solely profit-driven or unclear about their mission in the world (Higher Purpose)
- Because groups who have a high degree of autonomy in an environment where it is safe to be altruistic will experience a high degree of intrinsically rewarding, fulfilling work outperform groups who are centrally controlled and have minimal fulfillment from work (Conscious Culture)

So what is the job of Conscious Leadership? Creating the right set of conditions for all of the above to take place.

"Conscious managers exercise a minimum amount of control. Their role is not to control other people, it is to create the conditions that allow for more self-management."
(Mackey and Sisodia, 2013, 249).

This is not just a thing millennials like to have in their workplace today. This concept is more than 1000 years old, as exemplified by Lao Tzu's quote at the beginning of this section from around 6th Century BCE. This saying is generally attributed to Lao Tsu also known as Laozi who may have been an historic individual or this could be from a collection of wisdom assembled at that time under that name. When you get it right your people will be doing it themselves.

I saved leadership for last because it is up to leadership to encourage everything we have covered so far and to hold space for the other three principles: Culture, Purpose, and Stakeholder Orientation. As Stanley McCrystal writes, leadership is not commanding or directing. It is more like gardening: "Creating and maintaining the teamwork conditions we needed—tending the garden—became my primary responsibility" (McChrystal, 2015, 226).

Leadership does not need to come from nor should it come from one person. We humans were designed by evolution to work in mildly hierarchical environments. We don't like being told what to do, that interferes with our autonomy and intrinsic reward system. We were also designed for an environment in which leadership is fluid. If today the fish are running and we have decided we are going fishing and you are the best fisherperson, we will all be following your lead. If, on the other hand, we need to make some more spear points today because most of them broke on the mammoth hunt that Urg led a few days ago and I am the best at selecting and knapping stones into sharp spear points, then I will probably take the lead. Of course in reality in our tribal groups of 50 to 150 people, there will be multiple groups who self-organize around whatever needs doing and multiple people leading those efforts.

In today's environment, the organization should still be very similar. However, there are two instances where we may need one person as the designated "Leader." Because of the traditional business environment and the expectations of work that we now have, we need protecting from those old habits and assumptions. We need someone to assert the new, more human system and prevent the old system from re-asserting itself and taking over again. A business is like a multicellular organism. It has an immune system, and those white blood cells will sense that some foreign DNA has entered and will seek to stamp it out. There will also be powerful forces from outside the organization pressuring it to conform to business norms of hierarchy, strategic plans, budgets, and many of the other business artifacts we are used to. The other instance is in interacting with the world outside the company. Society expects that a company will have a president. Someone who can officially sign documents for the group.

This is how W.L. Gore is organized. There is no fixed hierarchical structure, leaders emerge. The only official leadership positions are established for required interactions with the outside world.

We need someone to protect the principle of autonomy and hold the space open to encourage us to bring our whole unique selves to work. Our unique personalities and perspectives are important assets for the group. They need to be present for the group to perform well. The leader holds space for intrinsically rewarding contributions. She does this by minimizing hierarchy, creating a psychologically safe environment, and highlighting the group's purpose.

Everyone getting group input for every decision every time something needs to be done is highly inefficient (meatloaf brain) and wastes valuable resources. Therefore, a strictly "flat" system of leadership among all members would not be ideal.

Central control is also inefficient. It takes too much time for information to get to central command and then for a decision to be made and passed back down through the organization. By the time the decision arrives, the situation has changed and it's likely that important information got lost along the way. Flexible leadership is the most efficient. The people who are best at and most engaged in the thing we are trying to do take the lead in that moment.

We were designed to live in mildly hierarchical environments where leadership is context-specific. This means it's about taking turns, based on what's right for a given situation. In a high-performing group, leadership is not fixed, it is fluid. The best person to lead in the present circumstances should be leading. Intuitively, of course, this makes sense. Maybe you're leading at this moment, but later you need to step aside and let someone else offer their leadership. This can be very hard (nearly impossible) for people whose self-worth is positional. This is one of the reasons so many organizations fail to transform themselves. An organization can only reach the level of maturity of its leader.

Gary Hamel on Leadership:

Ideally, everyone is leading from wherever they are in the organization. As David Marquet (2013) says in his book, *Turn the Ship Around*, instead of having one person (the submarine commander) telling 134 people what to do, it is better to have 135 people thinking about what needs doing and telling each other what they intend to do, asking questions if needed, and then just doing it. Progress and action at the speed of thought instead of the speed of chain of command, committee, or bureaucracy. If your competition is operating at the speed of thought and you are not, you are in big trouble.

David Marquet, former submarine commander, on leadership:

A FEW MORE THOUGHTS ON LEADERSHIP ...

BOOK REFLECTION

An Everyone Culture: Becoming a Deliberately Developmental Organization by Robert Kegan and Lisa Laskow Lahey, 2016

This book is by two Harvard organizational psychologists who go out in the field to research what they call Deliberately Developmental Organizations, or DDOs. These are companies that invest much more time and energy in their people's development than most companies. It is also their central focus every day. DDOs do this because they know it is essential for the people and the company to grow. Focus on development is what has created their success.

There is no tension between investing in the growth of their people and being profitable. It is one and the same thing for these companies. In Decurion, a company illustrated in this book, Christopher Forman says "We do not see a trade-off, and the moment we consider sacrificing one for the other, we recognize that we have lost both." (Kegan 2016, 96)

"BETTER ME + BETTER YOU = BETTER US" (Kegan 2016, 20)

Each of the companies used as an example in the book is a deliberate system that is all about growing people. As a consequence, the company also does extremely well.

If you ask people in one of these companies whether they focus on the development of their people because it is the right thing to do or because they believe it is the best thing for the organization, people will look at you funny because for them it is a non-question. It's both/ and. The two go inextricably together.

Kegan and Lahey offer engaging stories about each company. I encourage you to read them. Each company has unique ways in which it goes about consciously and deliberately engendering the development of everyone who works there. Even the leaders are not exempt from the process they have set up.

Most of us are familiar with the concept of child development. We know that children grow in capabilities. At one point, kids like to play Peek a Boo. It is because they have recently discovered what Piaget called "object permanence." Before this stage, things are just there sometimes and not there other times. When our brains figure out that the thing is now somewhere else but still exists, that's object permanence. We take great delight in covering our eyes and everything is gone and then uncovering our eyes and it is still there! How exciting!

Adults can grow. Around the age of twenty-five, our frontal cortex is nicely formed. The wiring of this part of our brain begins in our teenage years and continues until our early twenties. Our brains develop so slowly precisely so that they can be wired for our particular societal norms. That's an evolutionary adaptation for creatures living in complex societies. During these years we are being socialized into our culture's environment by parents, friends, and teachers. This results in what Kegan and Lahey call the socialized mind. This is the young person who may have just started working in their first job. They are working out what is expected of them and how they can fit in. Kegan and Lahey describe this using the terms *team player, faithful follower, aligning, seeks direction*, and *reliant* (Kegan 2016, 62 Figure 2–4)

The next level that most of us get to is the self-authoring mind. At this level, we become more conscious; we wake up and realize that we have been socialized into our worldview and it is not really our own. Sometimes this starts to happen in our forties as a midlife crisis that gives us a kick. We go on a hero's journey to discover meaning and purpose and create our own view of reality. This is called the self-authoring mind. This is a journey to discover our own best way to understand the world. We use this perspective to change our environment. These are the terms used to describe people in this stage: *Agenda driven, learns to lead, has their own compass, own framework, problem-solving*, and *independent* (Kegan 2016, 62 Figure 2–4). While having our own compass and framework is better than being unconscious of the societal framework we were living in, it can be limiting. It can be hard for people at this stage to hear information contrary to their personally developed worldview.

A very few of us get to the stage Kegan and Lahey call the self-transforming mind. At this stage, we become aware that there are many other frameworks out in the world and that many of them are more complete and may work as well or better than our own. We begin to shrug off the limitations of our own self-authored framework and explore these other frameworks. This is a journey to discover many best ways. We use a framework to examine other worldviews and continuously recreate our own framework to better reflect what we are learning. This stage is described in these terms: *meta leader, leads to learn, multi-frame, holds contradictions, problem-finding, interdependent.* (Kegan 2016, 62 Figure 2–4)

If you are fluent in Conscious Capitalism, you may have heard that an organization can't progress beyond the consciousness level of its leader. The three levels above show how true this is. I am going to exaggerate the descriptions below just a bit to make it clearer. In reality, it is usually not so black and white.

At the level of the socialized mind, a company leader may be doing what they were taught in business school or as part of an MBA program. They are following the social norms for running a business, checking off all the boxes on the "how to run a successful business list" that they were taught. If a person is at a supervisory or manager level, they will likely be acting just like their first manager or supervisor did. That is the model they are following.

Hopefully at some point they wake up. Maybe it is a midlife crisis. They get to their forties and they ask, "Is this all there is? Is making money what it is all about?" Maybe they have been treating their people like they are merely a resource and they have a conversion experience where they realize that each of these people is someone's precious child, just like their own son or daughter. They begin to rethink what they were taught and "self-author" their own worldview, based on their own values. Their company begins to run much better. More people engage in their work. The company discovers values and possibly even a purpose beyond profit.

As time goes by, some leaders who are now comfortable in their self-authored worldview become confident enough to feel safe (and even excited by) exploring alternative views. They realize that their self-authored view, their secret sauce that gave them success, is now probably holding them and their company back. They realize that the world is a lot more complex than they once thought. They realize that they must begin continually trying new things. They find joy in exploring possibilities and encourage others in their organization to do the same. They go way beyond their once-accepted way of doing work. They encourage others to lead from wherever they are and explore their own leadership views. They seek to continually recreate a framework that can be used to understand the other frameworks. Their own drive comes from a deep desire to learn, and they want everyone else in their company to learn and grow also. Ultimately, they understand that all of these realities are our own creations, and therefore, we are free to create new, more beautiful realities for people to enjoy.

Kegan and Lahey share evidence to suggest that the higher the level of development of the company leader (and therefore others in the company), the better the company's performance/tends to be.

Of course, this book is just another framework with which to look at ourselves, our businesses, and the world. I think it is a useful one. It certainly rings true to me as a person who loves learning new ideas and seeing how they fit with my current understanding.

Also, it seems that many of us are operating at one level in one area of our lives and at different levels in different areas of our lives. It could be more a matter of how much time we spend thinking at a particular level. For me, this indicates that it may not be so much a stage of development as it is a situational subjective worldview that is holding us back, particularly in our work lives.

If you would like to listen to a podcast in a similar vein, I suggest the Conscious Capitalist podcasts at https://www.theconsciouscapitalists.com/, especially #24, "Values and Consciousness with Richard Barrett," and #26 "Leaders Get the Organizations They Deserve," *which explores the journey to Conscious Leadership.*

BOOK REFLECTION

Mismatch: How Our Stone Age Brain Deceives Us Every Day (and What We Can Do About It) by Ronald Giphart and Mark van Vugt (2018)

The following are some ideas I gleaned from *Mismatch*, a book co-authored by writer Ronald Giphart and evolutionary biologist Mark van Vugt. The book is about the mismatch between the environment in which we were "designed" by evolution and the environment in which we now live and work. One section is about the mismatch in our work environment. Another section is on leadership.

The way we humans now lead our organizations in a positional hierarchical system is a mismatch for our human nature. One example of a different leadership system from their book is horse leadership.

Within herds of horses the leader is a mare. She is the leader because the other horses choose to follow her, they select her to lead them because she is the best at looking after the others, and she is the best at keeping the group healthy. She does not take leadership, it is given to her by the other horses.

This is the way Giphart and Vugt define leadership: "Leadership is a process of social influencing, whereby a leader coordinates the activities of one or more followers" (p159).

There is also a stallion and he does not lead, he follows. He guards the back of the herd and protects it from predators.

Gorillas establish "leadership" based on who is strongest. The strongest male gets all of the females. This is of course not real leadership according to the definition above. It is just dominance.

Chimpanzees will have none of that. If one male chimpanzee is too dominant and taking advantage of things for his own interest, several other male chimpanzees will gang up on him and put an end to it. This keeps dominance in check. No individual is stronger than the group.

In Bonobo groups, the females work as a group to keep males in check.

For humans, group survival is the key to passing along our genes (the goal of evolution, our "designer," is gene replication). Human cooperation is our main survival mechanism. Anything that gets in the way of cooperation (like aggressive and dominant individuals) needs to be eradicated. In our ancestral environments, the followers selected the leader(s). We did not have just one leader who led all the time. Leadership was fluid. Who was leading us depended on what was needed at that moment. The one most suited for that need took the lead.

Our current corporate structures do not allow for this flexibility. We do not select who will lead us. Leadership does not easily change when the situation changes. In addition, because managers are often "leading" from positional authority rather than being selected by their followers, their followers cannot easily get rid of them when they begin to behave in ways that are in their own interests instead of the interests of the group.

We could learn something from horses and our human ancestors. Two different species evolved similar solutions that work.

LORD OF THE RINGS LEADERSHIP STYLES

I am a Lord of the Rings fan.

I think the lesson from the books written by J. R. R. Tolkien is not the usual claim that power corrupts and absolute power corrupts absolutely. The lesson is that it is critical to pick the right leaders.

We tend to hire managers who are like Boromir was early in the story. We are attracted by their conviction and can-do attitude. We think that here is a natural leader, the person who can lead the charge into battle. Unfortunately, these people are less likely to take the time to see the whole picture, and too often they are attracted to power and glory.

Frodo offered the ring to Gandalf and he refused it. Galadriel and Aragorn also turned it down, as did Faramir. The same theme comes up in Harry Potter. Harry does not want to be sorted into Slytherin house; he is not interested in power and glory. He gets the Sorcerer's stone from the mirror of Erised (desire spelled backwards, as it would appear in a mirror) because only someone who wants to find the stone but does not want to use it for selfish purposes can get it.

We really should be promoting the people from within our organizations who are like Aragorn, Galadriel, Gandalf, and Faramir. People who really don't want the job. Humble leaders who put the care of others before themselves. People who know it is really the hobbits in their organization who get the work done and deserve all the help they can be given. The people doing the work are deserving of the praise.

True leaders kneel before their people. The leaders we need are those who will sacrifice themselves for the sake of the people they lead. We need to avoid choosing leaders who want power and position.

PART 2

CHAPTER 8

The Paradigm

We act according to our beliefs about ourselves and others. Creating shared worldviews is our superpower. An altruistic, purposeful self-view and worldview leads to individual and business success and (bonus points!) happiness, at both the individual and the group level.

We have been designed by group-level evolution to be altruistic. Our brains reward us with happiness when we have the autonomy to choose to do the things that benefit our groups.

We can't help being the unique individuals that our genes and experience made us. We need to value that uniqueness; our groups depend on it. Autonomy is the key to releasing this potential and to enabling the intrinsic rewards our brains are designed to give us.

Worldviews and systems that believe and reward us as if we were rational, value-calculating, and self-interested are false and destructive.

The conscious leader's mission is two-fold. To make her workplace and her larger business ecosystem safe for altruism by preventing, correcting, or removing selfish behavior, and by engendering maximum autonomy and minimal hierarchy.

Hopefully what you have read has convinced you that the paradigm above is true and you are eager to see examples of implementation.

IMPLEMENTATION

This is the second half of the book where we get practical. I am sharing my personal experiences. We will see why ideas like "change management" are idiotic.

There is an African proverb that states, "if you want to travel fast go alone, if you want to travel far go together." Well … sort of. There is a third option that is the best of both worlds. If you want to travel far and fast, go in a bunch of small groups.

Humans are meant to function best in small groups. Give the groups the mission and let them go.

A classic mistake that is made when attempting to change a large organization is to try to plan it all out and then do a little bit everywhere in the organization. Once that step is done, do a bit more, and so on. This is the standard command-and-control machine thinking and it does not work. The problem is that you are only going to go as fast as the slowest part of the organization. The faster, more eager parts will give up and become demoralized because they are totally bored by how slowly it is going. You are not going for uniformity, you are going for the fastest possible improvement.

The far better strategy is to explain the overall goal and then encourage experiments. You could begin by explaining the idea of intrinsically rewarding purposeful work and autonomy, for example. If a lot of groups get the idea and are enthusiastic, you are off to a good start. Encourage groups to try whatever they think will work for them and to share what they are doing with other groups.

What you want is an evolution based system of variation, sharing, selection, and replication of the things that are working. At the same time, be mindful that some things will be situationally and group dependent and will not work or will need to be adjusted by other groups.

Don't try to control it. Your role is to be coach and advisor. You are tending a garden that wants to flourish. You are holding the space for high-performing human systems to emerge. It will tune and prune on its own.

If there is reluctance to seize the opportunity to try new things, don't fret about it. Continue to explain what you hope will happen. You will surely find one small group someplace that wants to give it a try. Start there. It is better to do a whole lot with a small part than to try to do a little across the whole organization.

Remember, people have been socialized to do what they are told from a young age. (As Seth Godin says, that's what schools are for.) Just because you throw open the cell doors to the prison, don't expect everyone will be eager to come out into the sunlight. Many people have never been outside before. It may take time.

In our favor, we have the fact that humans are designed for this. We will come around, given time and the courage to trust the process. We will learn to be the high-performing, self-organizing, self-managing systems we naturally are.

So if you are thinking this sounds good, you probably want to see what it looks like in the real world. Spoiler alert: It looks even better!

CHAPTER 9

Sharing Info on Profitability in Real Time

Information sharing shows trust and enables autonomy. What can show more trust and what can be more useful than sharing profitability information? So that's what we did.

We had an ERP (Enterprise Resource Planning) system. It was typical of the software sold to most companies for running their business. It was designed to provide useful information to purchasing, sales, and especially accounting. How is it that these systems are not designed to help manufacturing, which after all is doing the work of changing the form, fit, and function the customer is actually paying for? Valuable information is closely held and guarded in these systems. Typically when implementing systems such as these, manufacturing and service work are held in thrall to the system instead of the other way around.

Like most of them our ERP system was garbage when it came to providing actionable manufacturing information, so we created our own system. It was surprisingly simple! This is what we did:

We wanted to get real-time information to the operators on how they were doing. Not to beat them up, but to share info. I likened it to a computer game. How engaging would it be to play an online game and never see a score? What if you got your score in an email a month later mixed in with a buch of other's scores as a composite average? That is what an ERP system does.

There are only a few things that matter: the raw material cost, the cost of processing, and the selling price. The first and last are easy.

To figure out the cost of processing was not much harder. If, for example, the total cost to run your business—sales, customer service, warehouse, production, etc., absolutely everything—is ten million dollars per year and you have ten machines that run the same product at the same rate and they run three shifts five days a week, then they are each running 6,000 hours a year and there are ten of them, so that's 60,000 hours of run time. The cost to run them per hour is ten million divided by 60,000 or $166.66 per hour.

But we all know it is not a perfect world and you probably have a variety of machines that are more or less expensive and take up more or less space on the production floor and have more or less operators and run more or fewer hours. But still it's not a really big problem. You can probably already come close to a good number for each machine in your head. Machine X is twice the capacity of machine Y, so that means that, if our average is $166.66 per hour, maybe machine X costs twice as much per hour as machine Y. But machine X runs twice as often as machine Y, so in reality their cost per hour is the same.

If your company is like ours, what you are going to find out is that your management overhead is the expensive part. The operators actually making the product are only about six to eight percent of the total cost. This is why, in my opinion, it is silly to try to save money on operators' pay rates when that is such a small contribution to overall costs, and good, engaged operators are way more productive, so they should be paid much more. But, I digress ...

The point is that it is not so hard to come up with a cost per hour to run each machine. Once you have that, you have everything you need.

You can import from the ERP system the cost of each raw material into Excel. You then set up a macro to do the following: The employee has just completed a batch. She enters in the product code number for the product she made, the time it took to make it, and the pounds produced.

The macro runs; it looks up the raw material costs based on the product code and calculates the total raw material cost based on the quantity of each one used. It looks up the cost per hour for the machine and multiplies that by the number of hours the operator entered. It looks up the average selling price of that product for the last X months (also imported from the ERP system). Average selling price – (RM cost + cost per hour of machine time) = profit!

Now your accounting department will tell you it's not perfect. But don't let perfection stand in the way of good enough. (Especially if they can't or don't have the time to do perfect for you!)

To keep the Excel files from getting messed up, we created an Access database operator interface so the operator would only see the fields he needed to see to enter information and get feedback. There was a field for the product code number, the lot number, the raw material total pounds consumed, the time, and the product yield in pounds. The access database also retained the information on each batch, which we used in our process improvement meetings as you will see.

Now you have immediate feedback. Informal competitions may ensue between shifts, or people may just be happy trying to improve their own score. This is where a supervisor can really become a coach. You may also find you have some wildly profitable products you didn't know about and you will probably find some real miserable ones. Not the operator's fault, but the pricing department just did not take into consideration that a particular product has a long drying time or some other pricing oops. Well at least you know about it now.

Remember autonomy and intrinsic reward? To work, this must be a good game. One of the essential qualities of a good game is that the player must opt in. This comes from *Reality Is Broken* by computer game designer Jane McGonigal (2012). (I highly recommend this book.)

How can work be more like a good game? According to McGonigal (p21), You need four things for a good game:

1. The goal is the specific outcome that players will work to achieve. It focuses their attention and continually orients their participation throughout the game. The goal provides players a sense of purpose. The best goals at work are the ones people and groups choose for themselves (maximize autonomy).

2. The rules place limitations on how players can achieve the goal. By removing or limiting the obvious ways of getting to the goal, the rules push players to explore previously uncharted possibility spaces. They unleash creativity and foster strategic thinking.

3. The Feedback System tells players how close they are to achieving the goal. It can take the form of points, levels, a score, or progress bar. Or in its most basic form, the feedback system can be as simple as the player's knowledge of an objective outcome: 'The game is over when ....' Real time

feedback serves as a promise to the players that the goal is definitely achievable, and it provides motivation to keep playing.

4. Finally, voluntary participation requires that everyone who is playing the game knowingly and willingly accepts the goal, the rules, and the feedback. Knowingness establishes common ground for multiple people to play together. And the freedom to enter or leave a game at will ensures that intentionally stressful and challenging work is experienced as safe and pleasurable activity.

How does this work in a manufacturing setting?

1. Goal: make as much good product as you can. This could be you personally, your whole team, shift or company, or all of the above.

2. The product must pass quality standards, customer needs, and expectations.

3. As soon as each batch is done you know how you did, and you can track your progress and other participating operators progress over time.

4. Operators must opt in. This can't be mandatory! Remember to be intrinsically rewarding we need to have the autonomy to participate or not. This is not about making more product. That would be a selfish motivation on the part of the company. This is about making work more engaging, which is an altruistic motivation on the part of the company. As a byproduct more and better quality product may ensue! Individuals and teams who do well can share their strategies with others. Teaching and sharing is intrinsically rewarding. This is just for fun, or bragging rights don't extrinsically reward this!

Notice how similar these four things are to the Prosocial Core Design Principles?

What can be changed in your workplace to make people's tasks and responsibilities more like part of a good game? What would it be like if we thought of maintenance and sanitation as taking on quests instead of work orders? Notice how demotivating the term *work order* is. How could we approach R&D, customer service, production, and scheduling more like a good game?

CHAPTER 10

Process Improvement Meetings

So, if you implemented an immediate feedback system to provide operators profitability information, you now have a database of very useful information. At our company, we held process improvement meetings to look at the data we were gathering. We would select one or two products to look at each meeting. We had about 750 different finished goods. We focused on the larger-volume products because, if we were losing money on something that we only ran on one machine for a few hours a year, fixing it (or not) was not going to make much difference. However, the larger-volume products would probably require the same investment of time to improve but make a larger impact.

We would signal what product we were going to review at the meeting and invite whomever wanted to participate. Operators, supervisors, managers, R&D people, purchasing, and even accounting showed up at the meetings. We reviewed the data on a large screen in the conference room and discussed it.

Sometimes we had a large-volume product that was marginally profitable. Despite our best efforts, we only managed to improve it just a bit, from an average of $150 per batch to $200 per batch. At other times, we had quite profitable products of $2,000 per batch that we could easily improve to $3,000 per batch by improving our process. Obviously from a company profitability perspective, we should focus on the latter instead of the former.

Everyone had perspective and information to share. It was a group effort in egalitarian meetings. Many things that came up were eye openers.

As an example, one raw material (RM) came in from several different suppliers. The particle size was very important. For our product to meet spec, the RM needed to fall into a particular range. Some suppliers were inconsistent, and we had costly reworks due to that. The correlation between our finished product specification failures and inconsistent suppliers was not evident until we gathered the data and met as a non-judgemental, non-hierarchical team to figure it out.

We discovered through experimentation that one product could be processed twice as fast and be a better product at the same time. In another case, when we looked at wildly differing processing times, the operator explained that the raw material came in different packaging. When it came in bags, it was easy to open and load. When it came in boxes, it took longer to open the boxes and pull out the poly liner inside. Far worse was when the same raw material came in small drums with lead crimp-on seals.

QA rightly did not want the lead seals on the drums when they came to the loading platform in case lead should fall into the product (food and potential lead contamination is not a good combination!). This required operators to unstack the pallets of drums outside the production room, cut off the seals, and then restack the drums on pallets before they could be placed on the loading platform. This dramatically increased the overall production time. The drums came from one of the more inexpensive suppliers, but when we looked at the overall picture, we could see they were the most expensive option. Because this opportunity for improvement had surfaced, purchasing changed their supplier contracts for future orders. Switching that one supplier away from drums to bags also reduced our waste stream, which was an environmental win at the same time.

CHAPTER 11

Start-of-Shift Meetings

At Watson, we ran twenty-four hours a day, six days a week. We used to do our start-of-shift meetings just like most companies. The supervisor would come in early to meet with the previous supervisor and then walk the facility to see what was going on for herself. She would then go to the start-of-shift meeting and tell her people what machine they had been assigned to, what that machine was running, who they would be working with, and what was expected of them that day. Standard workplace stuff.

We changed all that. We asked the question: How much autonomy can we create here? In the new process, operators chose the machine they wanted to run and who they wanted to run it with (Prosocial CDP #7). Each shift worked out their own system to fairly allow this to happen (CDP #3). There was a 30-minute shift overlap. operator teams would go out to the machine they had decided to run and talk to the operators of the previous shift to find out what they were doing and how it was going. Then they would come back to the start-of-shift meeting. When the group was assembled, each team took a turn sharing any important information (we are waiting on the warehouse for more raw material, the raw material looks different, the machine is making a noise, or everything is running well) and then tell what they intended to accomplish that day. In the new system, the supervisor is now a coach and scrum master. *Scrum master* is an Agile term. In an Agile system, a scrum master is someone who, among other things, helps remove obstacles for their group. It is her job to get the material from the warehouse, investigate the unusual noise with maintenance, and work with QA on any quality issues. A maintenance person would also be at the start-of-shift meetings to find out what was happening on the production floor.

Consider how just this one change made work so much more engaging. Each day I would ask myself if there is anything else we can do to create more autonomy. Ideally, people should be freely choosing what they are going to do, how and when they are going to do it, and who they are going to do it with. They should also have a strong feeling for *why* they are doing it. That *why* may come from their own sense of personal purpose or from the company or both (CDP#1).

Immediately after this meeting, we held the maintenance start-of-shift meeting. Maintenance mechanics gathered in a circle in the shop and shared what was happening on the floor. We then went around the circle with each mechanic saying what they intended to do that day. Someone volunteered to work on each of the pressing issues on the production floor. I never once had to assign anyone any work. People bravely took on assignments they had never tried to do before (feeling psychologically safe to try something new and possibly fail). Others volunteered to help them if they needed help or gave coaching tips during the meeting: "I would check this first. It is located in X room and looks like Y; if it is Z then I would check this next; let me know if you need help" and so on.

CHAPTER 12

Gratitude Round

This idea was covered earlier. I want to mention it again for your further consideration. Here it is illustrated in a different context in this example that my son sent me. He does a better job of explaining it and provides some interesting ways it can be done.

> *Hi Pop,*
>
> *I got an idea from LARP that you might be interested in. It lines up with your surprise rewards thing. (LARP is Live Action Role Play, improvisational theater where the actors/players are also the audience.)*
>
> *At the end of each LARP session, we wrap up the game and finish narrating the last stuff, and then each player nominates two people who they thought did good roleplaying, or who was especially helpful as a player. They say the name of the player, and then optionally tell what that person did that was awesome. For example, I might nominate Derek because he took time out of playing the game to help me create*

a character. And then nominate Skye because he did this really crazy thing in character and acted it well. Each player can also give honorable mentions if they thought that more than two people did really well, but you can only give two nominations.

After all the players have given their nominations, the story-teller (person in charge) will announce who won the "player's choice" award—the person who got the most player nominations. Each story-teller also gives a "storyteller's choice" award for good roleplay, often choosing the person with the second most nominations but just as often picking someone who was barely nominated because their good roleplay was done away from the group at large. And they tell the story and give their reasons for giving the award to that person.

So each person who got an award gets one extra experience point for that game, which is a pretty minor thing. Most of the time it doesn't even matter. But being given the award feels good, and being recognized by your peers feels good. You never nominate yourself, so you're getting two opportunities to tell others that you appreciate them and think they did well, which also makes you feel good because you're giving something. It also encourages everyone to think well of each other, and reminds everyone what good things they and everyone else did. Since everyone nominates two people, the chances are good that someone will nominate you at least sometimes, so you get that warm glow. Since the reward is so small, you never really feel upset at someone for getting it (it is an extra thing anyway, you don't need it). And because people have to explain why they nominate you don't get favoritism or bias as much.

So it occurred to me that there might be a place for this at Watson. At the end of the week, or the month, or a project, you could have the group of people meet up (this can't be the whole of Watson because it would take too long so you'd have to section out groups). People can nominate each other for having gone above and beyond, used their talents especially well, spent extra time, come up with an especially good solution, caught a problem before it became one, or helped someone out *when they weren't required to—that kind of thing. And then you could have the people's choice award and the supervisor(s) award(s) get a small bonus, like maybe twenty dollars bonus pay or a visa gift card or something like that, with the amount depending on how often you did this. It should be large enough that people feel like they got something, but not so large that people will actually covet it or hope for it in a big way. The meeting should happen when people can still remember what everyone did, so a month might be a bit long.*

Just an idea. I feel like in LARP it encourages people to do well because they get rewarded when they do by recognition. And when someone does well or helps you out you get to tell that to everyone in a space that's meant for that sort of thing, and if you help out behind the scenes that gets told to everyone as well so it actually recognizes people who do all kinds of work and isn't just a popularity contest. And it brings everyone in the group together, even if they hadn't been working together in close quarters, so that they find out the most awesome parts of what everyone else has been doing. Plus it encourages thinking outside the box, because people recognize it when you do that and often nominate you for it.

Also occasionally if we have a mitigating circumstance where we all did really well, or we had to meet up one less time this month and the storyteller wants to give us all a bonus, they can do that and say that we all get the award, but we're going to do nominations anyway (no one gets a double reward at that point so nominations are just to tell people you appreciated what they did). So if like everyone has been working overtime and you're really pleased with them and stuff then this provides a way to reward that too. But the everyone-awarding shouldn't be done too often or it would be expected and that defeats the purpose.

Just wanted to let you know in case it could be useful to you. I feel like sharing like this brings people closer together and lets people who have been helped "pay back" the person who helped them a bit, and lets people who do good work in private or in public get noticed and appreciated for it. The presence of the small reward means that people take the nominations seriously, but don't get upset when the nomination goes to someone else. Everyone isn't required to nominate two people, they just can choose to, but nearly everyone chooses to every time.

We also sometimes nominate in advance—if my character gave another character a difficult time, or if a character has been given a really difficult task to do and I know they'll be having a tough time coming up and need a bit of extra something to get through it, I could give them a nomination for that.

To clarify, if the nomination is for someone who had/is going to have a difficult time, then it's for someone who is stepping up to the challenge and taking it well—not complaining/being angry about it.

We usually have between fifteen and twenty-five people at a LARP, and with some people telling narratives and some people just saying names during nominations it feels about the right length of time to spend on the activity. More than twenty-five people, or too many people telling long narratives, I think would drag on too much.

Cheers,

Alex

CHAPTER 13

Compliments and Accomplishments Board

Another way of expressing gratitude and also sharing cool new stuff that was happening was our Compliments and Accomplishments Board. This was just a big white board and a lot of colorful markers in the lunchroom. Anyone who wanted to was welcome to write a compliment to someone or some group for everyone to see. Lots of people did this. We also used it to share significant accomplishments we had made. We were running four shifts, so this was one of the ways that people could keep up with what other shifts were doing or had done.

Sharing ideas among groups increases the likelihood of more and better ideas and engagement. Minimum control and maximum autonomy are key to creative experimentation.

IDEA PROCESS

We wanted to iterate ideas faster. I was always happy to hear ideas as I walked around the building visiting people and happy to greenlight them and provide resources. But what if I did not happen to pass by you as you had a hot idea? How could we do this more easily?

We created a wall to visually run the process. It was a bit like a scrum board mixed with an open space meeting and using the advice process. The first area was for posting ideas. We created a simple form for it. You wrote a sentence or two about the idea, along with your name, and posted it on the wall. People were free to look the ideas over, and anyone who thought an idea was good could write their name down in support. If you got enough support for your idea, you moved it down the wall to the Assessment area. In this stage, the idea got a more critical review and you could seek out advice from others engaged in that area. If the idea passed, it went on to the next stage and section of the wall, the Implementation section. After we tried the idea, we moved it to the final stage, Celebration. If it worked, we celebrated. If it did not work, we celebrated!

The idea is to try things and learn from them. Some things don't work, but what you learn along the way may be critical for something else to work. Celebration no matter what happens keeps the creative vibe going.

CHAPTER 14

Company Garden

My sister and I were working on ideas to save our people money. We were already working on paying our people as much as we could, so we asked ourselves, *How can we help people's pay go further?* The idea of a company garden emerged.

We asked around to see if people thought it was a good idea. We got positive feedback, so we plowed up about two acres of lawn in front of the warehouse. About 60 people (out of about 280) signed up for a garden plot. A garden committee of volunteers organized the plots and set up a fence. My sister had the soil tested, and we made the recommended pH adjustments to the soil to promote plant growth. The first year, we had a simple garden. Due to the success of it, we installed drip irrigation and ground cloth the second year. The third year, we plowed an additional acre.

The garden was divided into plots. We ordered plants and seeds as a group. The plants and seeds were delivered and gardening ensued.

People found themselves gardening next to others that they knew only by sight. People from different departments shared gardening tips and grew food and friendships. About 25 percent of the garden was designated for the local food bank. My sister engaged in a collaborative effort with a local school for kids on the autism spectrum. The kids tended the garden for the food pantry and took the produce down to the pantry. Anyone with an overabundance of produce from their personal garden also contributed to the food bank.

What started as a way to extend paychecks turned out to be an altruistic social experiment.

CHAPTER 15

Customers

A conscious company picks its customers carefully. Like all companies, we had those customers who were not all that interested in us and would switch to a different supplier for a few pennies. These also tended to be high-maintenance customers. Because they were focused on their bottom line and operating with a lot of central control and penny pinching, they were more likely to run out of ingredients and place rush orders, and they expected the world to revolve around them. The trick was not to give them more than their due attention.

We likened it to a car dealership. Most car companies have a luxury brand and an economy brand. If you buy the luxury car, you get the luxury treatment: a free loaner car for the day while yours is serviced, for example. If you buy the economy brand, you need to ask your friend for a ride to work.

Customers are similar. If they are the sort that is going to switch for a few pennies and have no loyalty, then they should get minimal service. Nothing personal, it's just business. That is the level they are operating on, so you should also unless you are convinced you can get them to play at a higher, less selfish, more altruistic level.

On the other hand, if customers really get you and you share a common sense of purpose, then it is an entirely different relationship. This is where it gets exciting.

I want to clarify that I am not just talking about good collaborative relationships. This is not only about finding win-win scenarios, though that is a part of it.

What I am excited about is real altruism. This is a relationship where you happily help each other out whether there is something tangible in it for you or not. In this sort of relationship, you will even happily pass along your customer to a competitor if you believe that competitor can serve them better.

We had such a relationship with a customer. They are a global consumer products company and the market leader in many of their categories. They were probably our most profitable customer, and we were one of their best and favorite suppliers. They told us several times that they no longer shopped around for the type of products we made for them; they just came to us. When we were not going to be the best supplier for them, our salesperson passed them on to a competitor, helped them make contact, and later followed up to make sure the project was going okay.

Our purchasing department and our customer's purchasing department routinely shared information about raw material suppliers and introduced each other to new suppliers of products each other needed. We were able to buy some of the ingredients we needed off of contracts they had negotiated at a much lower cost due to their larger size.

We openly shared our manufacturing process, including trade secrets, with them. We shared our R&D process, and we even gave them sets of our R&D equipment so they could do their own R&D

at their own facility. They in turn openly shared information about their business and R&D into new products and invited us into collaborative, co-development projects. We spent many days together running production trials on new products and evaluating them together.

This was a truly altruistic relationship. They are a great company with an excellent culture and friendly people. Our motivation was to see them succeed by doing what we could to help them.

CHAPTER 16

Kaizen Energy

In the terminology of lean manufacturing, the word *kaizen* means "change for the better." A kaizen event is a gathering of a few individuals for a limited period of time to study a process and improve it. Usually around six people work on a project for a week or so. Ideally the team is composed of people who work in that area, people who provide product or services to that group, people who receive product or services from that group, and people who know little or nothing about it to provide outside perspective.

If you are a manufacturing company, you may spend a significant sum on electricity and natural gas. This was the case for us. Altogether we spent about one million dollars every year on energy—about $750K on electricity and about $250K on natural gas. Most of this energy went into manufacturing.

Since 2010, I had been buying 100 percent renewable electricity from wind. It was only about 2 percent more expensive than regular electricity, and I felt it was well worth it. I have always been strongly motivated to save energy and reduce my carbon footprint. Maybe it was all those wasted hours as a 16-year-old in 1973, waiting in line for hours to get a few gallons of gas for our family's gas-guzzling Ford Montego wagon.

We had instituted a lean program in our company in 2013. We availed ourselves of a great lean sensei, Fred Shamburg. His company is Leanovations. They are located in Connecticut but Fred has worked all over the planet. Fred, along with the company Traver IDC, helped us do an energy kaizen event. The goal was to look at our manufacturing and building energy usage and discover and implement ways to reduce it.

When the work was completed, we had reduced our electricity consumption by 25 percent while the business grew 10 percent during the same 18-month time period.

I asked for volunteers from anywhere in the company. People put themselves forward to be on the energy kaizen team. Managers were negotiated with and people were freed up for the week's event. I was pleased to find so many people passionate about saving energy.

United Illuminating, our utility company, had a program called Energy Usage Assessment EUA. If we found and proposed energy savings in multiple areas, they would give us a larger energy incentive. If we only changed out the lights to LEDs, the incentive was about 20 percent. The utility wanted something more comprehensive. Our goal was to get the incentive to 50 percent, which we did. In total we spent just over $500,000 and the utility wrote us a check for just over $250,000. Our efforts paid for themselves in less than five years.

Most companies hire a consultant like Traver IDC to come in, do the assessment, and write up a report and submit it to the utility. This is okay and it is expedient. The downside is you are going to find less stuff, not get any additional engagement, and will have trouble maintaining success and making additional improvements.

Instead, we invited Traver to teach our people about energy saving and how to collect the information for the assessment. Our team fanned out across the building, gathering information on everything. When you have your own team doing this, they already know where many of the opportunities for improvement are and they ferret them out more completely. The team brought the information back to the conference room we had commandeered and entered the information into a spreadsheet. I was surprised by some of what I saw when we created graphics to display the information. One thing I had not realized was that our old air compressor was consuming 25 percent of the electricity we used. In the end, we replaced all of the building's lighting with LEDs, 35 rooftop AC units for more efficient ones, got a new VFD controlled air compressor, installed larger piping and a larger air storage tank for the compressed air, fixed about $30k worth of compressed air leaks, replaced old inefficient motors, replaced old dust collection systems, and fixed or replaced numerous broken steam traps.

If you are doing lean right, you will almost certainly end up on the doorstep of Conscious Capitalism. As Fred Shamburg says, lean is a "growth strategy." It is not about laying people off and saving money on labor. It is about finding ways to work more safely and effectively and to free people up to do things the company could not afford to do before, or creating more capacity so you can bring in more business without needing to buy more equipment or hire more people.

You might recall the shipwreck survival stories in Nicholas Christakis' book, *Blueprint*. Those shipwrecked groups who left people behind almost always failed to survive. The ones who went out of their way to take care of the sick and injured almost always survived.

If a company uses lean practices to cut people from the payroll, it is damaging its chances of survival.

Imagine you gather a group who do a particular part of a process every day and ask them to make the process more efficient. The group figures out how to rearrange the equipment and the process so that it needs only four people instead of five, and the fifth person gets fired. How many volunteers do you think you are going to get for the next kaizen event? Every company has positions it would love to create. We always wanted to have a parts department person. The parts room was usually a mess. We needed someone to fill the job of parts manager, but we did not have the resources to hire someone. During one kaizen event, we freed up someone. People were allowed to reshuffle themselves into jobs they preferred, and one of them became the parts manager. This was someone who was highly organized; you might have called him a neat freak, and he loved the new job. Everyone loved having a neat parts room and appreciated not running out of things we needed.

When you do Lean right, people have the chance to work *on* the business instead of *in* the business. You freely share the information people need. You are giving them the responsibility to take charge of an opportunity and trusting them to make improvements. You are empowering and possibly even emancipating them. Many people have never had this sort of experience before and they can become highly engaged. There is little chance of backsliding in any of the improvements being made, and there is a high probability of additional improvements happening in the future, even without a formal event.

Nothing made me happier than discovering that people had seen an opportunity for improvement and just done it. Optimal Lean is continuous improvement that does not need to be done in a formal way. The formalities are necessary when doing it for the first time.

They are, however, akin to training wheels and can be taken off as groups become engaged and see opportunities.

Agile, or Scrum, is the same sort of system. It is a framework that people can use until they no longer need it. Sometimes the framework is needed by people on the team who are getting used to more self-management. Sometimes the Lean or Agile framework is needed to preserve the team's autonomy by keeping managers and supervisors out of the team's way.

CHAPTER 17

Finding the Production Floor Rearranged

I used to enjoy coming in early to see the people working the night shift. This required me to get up at 4:00 am, which I did most days. The night crew was highly motivated. They had conscious supervisors, natural leaders who created a great culture. One morning I came in and found them particularly excited to see me. They wanted me to come see what they had been up to.

I walked out onto the production floor and was amazed by what I saw.

There had not been a lot to do that particular night. There was some production going on and some cleaning to do. Someone had pointed out that a particular machine was in the way of the process much of the time. Someone else pointed out that one of the production rooms was full of equipment that we did not use any more. Someone suggested that the room could be emptied and the equipment stored in the warehouse. Then the machine that was in the way could be moved into the emptied room, and that would actually be a better spot for it and then … ideas ensued.

The group decided the idea was just too good, so they decided to go for it. They got the warehouse forklift operators to help them move equipment, and they got maintenance to move wiring and other utilities. They tried a couple of arrangements of the equipment in the new locations. By the time I came in, a significant part of the production floor had been reorganized. It was awesome!

No one had asked for permission. No one had awakened the production manager or assistant production manager at 1:00 am to get their okay. They just did it. This is what moving at the speed of thought instead of moving at the speed of bureaucracy looks like. They all left work that day thoroughly exhausted and gloriously fulfilled.

CHAPTER 18

Open Space Technology

"There are no fancy management theories and it is not about hiring dream teams. It is just a matter of biology and anthropology. If certain conditions are met and people inside the organization feel safe among each other, they will work together to achieve things none of them could have achieved alone. The result is that their organization towers over their competition."
          —Simon Sinek *Leaders Eat Last*

Open space technology is not really a technology. That's just what it is called by its creator, Harrison Owen. It is really a way to have a self-organizing meeting and get a lot of stuff done.

This is how it works in a nutshell:

There is an opportunity or issue that needs to be addressed.

You let everyone know what the opportunity is and you tell them you are having an open space meeting with a date, time, and location. Anyone interested can come. No one is required to be there.

On the day of the meeting, people come to the place. They find a suitably large room with chairs arranged in a circle. When it seems the right time, the meeting commences.

The process is explained.

In the center of the circle of chairs is a pile of paper, some markers, and some tape. Anyone who has an idea related to the opportunity at hand can stand up, write it down in one or two sentences on a sheet of paper, and introduce it to the group. They then use the tape to post the idea on a wall already marked out in a grid of time slots and locations. After everyone who has an idea has had the opportunity to briefly share it and post it on the wall, the marketplace is opened.

The grid on the wall of ideas is the marketplace. Attendees "shop" the ideas and sign up to brainstorm or discuss any they like. Then he meetings ensue.

During the meetings, someone volunteers to take notes. We kept notes on very large Post-It sheets and then posted them on the "Newsroom wall" so others could see what had happened in that meeting. No one was in charge and everyone was.

As Harrison Owen says, "Whenever it starts is the right time. Whoever comes are the right people. Whatever happens is the only thing that could have happened" (Harrison 2008, 70). There is only one law of Open Space meetings. It is the law of two feet. If you are not feeling that you are making a contribution in a meeting, you can use your two feet to join a different meeting.

When we had these meetings, we went beyond the framework of Open Space. We took the outcomes from the Open Space meeting and adapted something similar to the Agile Scrum process. We gathered the large Post-It sheets from the Open Space meeting and put them up in a hallway near the process or department related to the event. There were always unfinished items that could not be completed during the open space meeting, for example reorganizing tools or process changes that needed to be formalized in change control documents. People wrote their name down next to those items they were interested in. This way anyone could see who was working on what. Teams formed spontaneously, composed of people who wanted to be involved. When an item was completed, someone would write "done" next to the item and people would resort themselves to tackle other items until everything was done.

If you have not seen self-organizing, self-directed teams of highly engaged people in action, prepare to be amazed. This is the real thing.

In my view this is who we really are as a species. Altruistic group creatures, intrinsically motivated to do the things we do best in support of our group. We are naturally gifted to see what needs doing and how we can best contribute.

Harrison Owen writes in his book, *Wave Rider*, "All human systems are self-organizing and naturally tend towards high performance provided the essential preconditions are present and sustained … High Performance is less a matter of doing something … but rather being fully and intentionally what we already are: a self-organizing system."

So let me set the scene for a day in an Open Space meeting. This is a true story; only the confidential names have been changed.

Opportunity = Customer One wants to launch a new product, which will require us to produce XX thousands of pounds of Y for them. This is one of our largest and most profitable customers. The equipment needed to produce this product would take about twelve months to order and install. We have no more space in the building, so an addition to the building is necessary. This customer loves us so much that they always come to us first and usually only buy this sort of product from us.

Issue = We appear to be out of capacity, and lead time to add additional machine capacity is much too long for Customer One.

Invitation to a meeting to discuss this is issued to all 300 people in the company. Anyone who is interested is welcome to attend.

Meeting Location = Offsite at nearby hotel

Intended start time = 8:00 am

Wednesday, July 8, 2015

At 8:10 or so we start (whenever it starts is the right time). Around thirty people have self-selected to participate. As mentioned above, everyone is sitting in a circle and my sister Mary, who is also the salesperson for this customer, reintroduces the opportunity and the issue.

Within a minute, it starts. One at a time people are introducing themselves and their idea for discussion and posting the ideas on the wall in time and space.

After fifteen minutes or so, everyone who wants to has proposed an idea and posted it on the marketplace wall. The marketplace is opened and people begin to sign up for meetings. There are no managers in these meetings; the majority of attendees are equipment operators and hands-on supervisors. In most instances, it is the operators who generate the ideas and lead the discussions.

See Appendix 1 for the list of what came from each meeting that day. Most of these suggestions were implemented in a few weeks. Some that required ordering new equipment took longer. Don't be concerned if you do not understand what these notes are all about; you would need much more context to do that. I encourage you to take at least a cursory glance at them, though, because what I want you to see is the sheer number of creative ideas and improvements that were generated during this one-day meeting. I expect you will be astounded.

All of the notes were originally gathered on large poster-size Post-It notes and posted in the hallway outside the processing rooms.

People signed up in groups of two and three to take care of the things the groups had decided needed to be done. When they were done, they wrote "done" next to the item and chose another one to work on.

There was no agenda. No one was told to come. All the ideas were freely given. Consensus was arrived at. Nothing was proposed by or approved by management. All tasks were self-assigned and accomplished. At no time did anyone tell anyone else what to do.

Yeah, it can be that good!

Some Final Thoughts

THERE ARE SOME BAD PEOPLE OUT THERE. WHAT TO DO ABOUT IT.

I was not born yesterday, and I know there are some really bad people out there. If you suspect you have a narcissist or a sociopath in your company, get rid of them as quickly as possible.

It is not your job to try to cure them; it is your job to protect your people. Don't let apparent stellar performance or excellent credentials get in the way of your decision. These people are masters at making themselves look good at the expense of others.

It is worth taking a few minutes and looking up information on narcissism and sociopathy. A quick Wikipedia search will give you some insight into these personality types. Like all personality attributes, people are on a continuum. Everyone is somewhere between Mother Teresa and Joseph Stalin. As a leader, you need to make the decision on where you will draw your line.

As Prosocial CDP number five states, start with a gentle reminder about appropriate, agreed-upon behavior, then gradually escalate sanctions from there. However, if you suspect an individual has a toxic personality disorder, do it more quickly and less gradually. You are responsible for the psychological safety of your group.

I had this sort of individual 5 times in a 25 year period, with an average of 150 people working for us during that time. In three cases, I interviewed and hired them. All of them were male. Each came across as an excellent candidate, very knowledgeable and compelling in their interviews.

The first turned out to be a pathological liar. I confronted him about several of the lies, and he stopped coming to work.

The second one said all the right things during the interview our HR manager and I conducted. As our HR manager said after the interview, "if he is half as good as he sounds he will be excellent." As it turned out he was what our HR manager later accurately named as a real chest thumper. He was awesome and everyone else was next to useless. Within a few days, we suspected we had made a mistake. Department morale sunk almost immediately, and we let him go after about a week. As far as he was concerned, we were making a huge mistake.

The third one was the worst. He enjoyed creating a toxic atmosphere. He was so destructive he drove one of our best, most compassionate and dedicated employees to tears. After we fired him, he sued us of course. Unfortunately he was stealthy and it took me a while to catch on. I then tried to work with him on his behavior and tried this for way too long. It is one of my biggest regrets that I did not fire him sooner. My slow response allowed him to cause so much pain and anguish in his department.

There were two others who were also bad, and eventually we realized we needed to let them go. Before firing them, we gave them professional management coaches to work on their issues, but as you might expect regarding an innate personality attribute, the coaching had no significant effect on their behavior.

Like all personality traits, these are on a continuum. Some people may be able and willing to change and others not. Your primary leadership duty is to the group. Roughly one in one hundred people are sociopathic.

OTHER INSTANCES OF PEOPLE NOT GETTING IT

If you are making a transition to a Conscious Company, there may be people who just are not fitting in. In some cases they may choose to leave on their own. Some people like positional authority. They are not going to be a good fit in an organization that is endeavoring to change to a workplace with a great deal of autonomy. Wish them well. There are plenty of opportunities out there for them.

Others may have a hard time getting used to having more autonomy themselves. Be patient with them; they have been raised in schools with clear rules and clear expectations and being told what to do. They have had work experiences with supervisors and managers who were all too happy to tell them what to do all day. Your new system is going to take some getting used to. Not everyone is going to want to come out into the sunlight as soon as you unlock the doors.

I, of course, appreciate energetic, highly engaged people, and I find that most people are this way. When people join a company, they are excited about their new job and have high hopes for fulfilling work. It is my job to create the conditions for that to happen. My goal is that eventually everyone gets there.

I have patience for the zombie sleepwalkers who are not engaged yet. I do my best to discover what interests them and help them find those opportunities where they can do what they do best for their group, and thereby become engaged. Better for them, and better for the rest of us in the company.

I even have patience for the people who are drilling holes. Goddess only knows what their lives have been like and what they are dealing with. I do my best to try to understand them and help them focus their discontent into a productive improvement for all of us.

What I will not tolerate is anyone who deliberately causes suffering. I have had people who took joy in mentally torturing others, and that is just not tolerable. I will also not tolerate anyone who seeks to cause strife and conflict on purpose.

Appendix 1

OPEN SPACE MEETING NOTES

From about 30 people in one day of collaborating.

To understand everything below, you would need a lot more context. I am sharing these notes not so you understand the details of what the group did, but because I want you to get an impression of what is possible in an Open Space meeting. I am sharing them because I expect you to be amazed.

These are the actual notes that I edited only to protect customer identity and confidential information:

Reduce Downtime for Making Solutions

Karina, Ivonne, Felicia, Elida, Wayne, Jack, Jacqueline, Amparo

The West Haven Warehouse is adding one more operator on second and one for third shift. This should get us kits on the platforms faster. I will speak to them about this also so they understand what we need. I think we should give them a chance to see if the extra two people solve the problem in West Haven.

They are also adding one more team to make kits in Orange. There are three teams now so this would make four teams. I think we need to give them a chance to see if this works to get us the kits we need on time.

Reduce Downtime for solutions, takes too long to come over from Orange Warehouse, and waiting on the forklift operator to bring the kit down or over.

1. Can other people get certified to use forklifts and know how to use the scanner for process pro. Or, have a dedicated forklift operator?
2. Being able to scan on the floor, like the lecithin, a log book that shows the product has been scanned. Could be the dedicated forklift operator does this.
3. We would like two to three days worth of kits on hand.
4. Unload the truck from Orange faster, rush products should go in the tail so that they get off loaded faster.
5. Could we deliver the film kits to the back door by the cutting room? Take advantage of this door being by the film area.
6. Investigate more how to improve getting the kits made on time.
7. Schedule kits better.
8. Product Y, change batch sheet order of events so that it is more efficient. For instance, overlap the RM C time with the cooling time. Product X seems to be the most drawn out, taking the longest, lease efficient (per Wayne).

9. Get a better, faster, more efficient way to mix the RM C and RM D because of the increase in volume, a second tank, stronger agitation. Follow up note from Gavin; I am working on getting a 120 gallon tank just like the sixty gallon tank we have now. This way we will be able to do X and Z products at the same time. We will also be able to mix the color for the fifty mesh in just two shots instead of four.

10. Scheduling, make the largest batch size possible. The other day we made four X 2000 lbs, gum arabic, why not make two batches of 4,000 lbs? This will save on quality checks and the batch would be more uniform.

Slitting room—Cutting

1. Make the core 1/4" wider for the 320 mm, right now it is just a bit too small, that makes it difficult to slit.

   Note from Gavin; Good idea we checked and unfortunately we can't do this, China customer needs it to be the way they are.

2. Film on roll that is going to the cutting room, think of it more as In Process, suspend rolls on a bar on a "C" shaped rack, use one long poly liner to cover the entire bar of rolls, close with a blue tie and a pallet marker.

3. Store C shaped racks, right by the cutting (maybe set up an area that these only fit in so that they have to be stored right outside the cutting room?).

4. Continue to label each roll, pull that label off to capture what has been done when they are used in the cutting room.

Quality—Reduce Rework

Have a supervisor check the product once per hour, reducing rework.

Have a custom sheet to capture and check the following:

- Shift
- Product running
- What to test
- Initially: Once per hour
- Have a picture of what the ideal should look like
- Sprinkle out glitter onto a piece of paper (or white plate like the black ones in the cutting room), make sure it is not wet
- Black Pantone check, on table outside of film production area with proper light so samples can be checked quickly and easily, don't need to go up to the lab
- Especially on WT—check the pantone for the first ten batches to establish the pantone range

We would need a different checklist for each product.

When there is an issue, the supervisor uses the opportunity for training, like the ... in product X ... the supervisor should not solve it themselves without the individual's involvement.

Retraining supervisors so that they understand quality is the most important, rather than just making a lot of product that will have issues.

There is stress in getting the orders out on time, it appears "good enough" or "don't worry about that, just get it out the door" is the message that the operators are hearing from some of the supervisors. We need a solution to this, with the increase in volume the stress is just going to increase.

Batch sheet—update, capture learnings, example, Product Y, what we learned when we just ran it will be forgotten in three months when we run it again.

Solution operators would like a conversion factor, X number of pounds of rework then add X amount of water for rework. This will make the rework faster because they will be able to add the right amount of water at the start.

Cross training—film line operators to the slitting room so that they know how important it is to communicate holes, lines on the film, other defects ….

Line two, need a second hose (used to have two), with more pressure. It is especially difficult to clean out after making Product Y when there is not enough water pressure.

New filter, line two, on the back wall of the wet end, bottom hose filter, for the UV light, when you turn it on water spews out.

Scheduling production

L.S. is going to start doing the film customer service and scheduling in November. People will work as a team to set the schedule to take care of orders and maintaining stock.

1. The people involved in scheduling need to see a visual of what really goes on in the production. Maybe they should spend some time in production?
2. Need to be more realistic, sometimes something is on the shipping schedule and it is not even made yet.

3. Schedule like products together, larger batches, longer runs.
4. Understand the production losses better so that we schedule the right size batches.
5. Rotate a film person in from time to time to cover the scheduling meeting.

10:00 Ken B, Ken, Jean, Wilfredo, Jack, Joe, James, Johnathan ….

Reduce production variation

1. Condition incoming hood air so that it is consistent and film runs faster. Working on this we are getting proposals for equipment to make more uniformly dry air.

   The air has a certain amount of moisture that it can hold. So in the winter, when the air is really dry it runs the fastest. In the winter we have been able to run an eighty fpm, in the summer this would not be possible. RH over thirty causes an issue on the film, water droplets form.

   Install a desiccated wheel.

   These units will heat the air as well which would be good for us.

   We have the names of four companies that make the units, one is coming on Tuesday, July 21, to see the production area.

Could have one for each line or one to cover the entire film area.

Might need to go on the roof, could weigh 6,000 to 7,000 lbs so we might need to add more support.

The dryer the air the better.

Can we tap off this conditioned air to be used in the cyclone, keep the glitter from sticking.

Can we slit directly off the line? This is more complex, how could we manage this?

Can we have a die that makes the 320 mm width? You would need a space between each one. It would have to be perfect since it is not getting trimmed.

Put a blue tie or shim between

Have a way to have the moisture meter track from side to side, like the thickness gauge, so that we know if the edges are wet.

Pumps, Mass flow meters, we have these in the trailer, three total (one is in pieces/parts). We started using one of these with the EM film on line two yesterday. We need to start recording the flow in liters per minute on the batch sheet somewhere and then have the lab update the batch sheets with that information.

Would need a chart that shows solution solids content, line speed, should be viscosity independent, basically a formula to do the calculation.

Robert said they have already been put in place on line one, but space is tight to put one on line two.

2. Set up line two so that we can make Z product and X product, need different wind up.

> How do we change rolls if we are going eighty fpm? Set up the second wind up toward the wet end, operators will need some practice to get this down. Right now we are making about one roll every hour, so at eighty FPM this would be a roll every thirty-five to forty minutes.

> Need a moisture meter for line two that is the same as we have on line one.

> Mass flow meter:

> Wind up/Take up, Ken B is working on setting this up, it will be closer to the wet end so we need to be careful that we are not too close to the stairs.

> Dust collection for the room when we are making glitter, keep the room cleaner which will save in clean-up time.

> Product Y, recycle, have it go in lower so it goes into the mill instead of flying around. Or put the mill under the cyclone? Keep it under negative pressure. Done.

> Film width for 320 mm cast the film width, we'll get three rolls from each line. We could get three rolls of twelve inches and one roll of five inches if we can manage this in the computer and lot control.

3. Make both solution rooms and line compatible so that any product can be run on either line. This would allow us to move a kit to the other line for flexibility.

Can we get larger/taller tanks to replace the smaller tanks?

If the product is already in the tank, and you want to move it to a different line, it would be good to be able to pump it to the other line. This would be good if one of the lines goes down and we need to switch the production to the other line.

4. Install tension control with eye, get technical support from the manufacturer.

5. Can we cut 320 mm into squares? This way we would only have one width.

6. Make Q's right off the line.

11:30, Jean, Bunchum, Karina, Ken,

Cut down batch time, Wasting time waiting for solution

1. Do the instructions need to be followed exactly?
2. Change the order of the steps, to be more efficient. Get the Titanium going first, since this takes the longest, then go to the other steps. RM M takes a long time too.
3. Clean when it is logical, clean multiple tanks at the same time.

4. Can RM C be added in sooner, do we have to wait until the batch cools down to level on the batch sheet, what is the max temperature that the RM C and M can be added at? They need to be added before the batch cools below 120F because the solution needs to still have a low enough viscosity that the C and M will mix in real well. Once the solution thickens up they may not mix evenly.

5. We would like to heat up the tanks faster, if some-one else is using steam in the other room then there is not enough steam to heat up the batch, so it takes longer than planned. Work is being done in the boiler room, will that help?

6. Cooling down, would be good if this can go faster too. Rework will also slow down the cooling process since it is too thick, better to add the right amount of water at the start, would be faster.

7. Mask and goggles for rework especially with Raw Material M.

8. Load the tanks with two people when we are in a rush.

9. Water pressure, not enough, especially if someone is washing on the other side.

10. Waiting on the forklift operator.

11. Schedule is not clear and changes too much, we don't know what to run and set up.

12. Need a second sixty gallon tank, used for C and D. Could there be better agitation to mix faster? Right now it takes a minimum of eight hours to make the RM C. The longer agitator worked better than the short one that is in there now. Or a double agitator would be good, one on the bottom, one on the top.

I am working on getting a second tank 120 gallons for Mixing RM C (The new tank has been ordered by Gavin).

13. Have solution operators be trained to drive the forklift, don't have to wait on anyone, go and get it when you need it. Have the solution operators write down the liquids they pulled from inventory, write it in a log book, then have someone else enter the data. The preference is not to have to scan it, there is concern that it might get scanned more than once, so by writing in a log and entering it as a separate step we always know what has been scanned. Having a dedicated fork lift driver for film would not be good, not a full time job, too much down time.

14. Control inventory better, inventory shows that the film group has it, but they don't. Have the solution operators scan the liquids they use, so it is more accurate and always gets done.

15. Better clamp to go around the lecithin drum, make it easier to pour out.

16. Schedule the solution room to always be ahead, but this only works if the production does not change so often. Right now they feel that everything has to be done last minute because the schedule changes so often.

Shift Changeover—Communication

White board to communicate, make sure you are also talking, the white board does not replace the conversation, it is just an extra tool.

There is enough time, just needs to get done.

Maintenance

Solution room #2, the agitator gets tripped, Maintenance has come in a few times but it is still not really fixed. Tom Stevens has been working on it. It trips.

Only one person knows Product X equipment, so X ends up waiting, need more cross training. Most of the time it is Kenny, need to have others that know the film area too.

There is no one who understands Product X on second and third shift.

Temperature gauge, important that this is accurate, Tom just fixed this.

Rework, How to reduce it

Solution room #1, need another plug, independent female connection for the mixing.

Extra electrical plug in the solution room, with this we don't need to have long extension cords going around.

Starting the line is difficult, better to have one person on the wet end and one on the dry line.

Conditioning the air = less rework.

Flow rate meter will help with color consistency since it should be more consistent for thickness.

Wash down, much better with two people since we have two hoses. Must have enough water pressure.

Ken B, Jean, Jack, Wayne, Ken,

Belt Tracking

Belt maintenance, how to check the belt, make sure they are square, make sure the tracking is right.

Before you start up a belt, make sure the belt is on the center of the drum.

Set tracking numbers at "12:30" (like a clock).

Run in automatic on both ends.

While you are running, watch these things:

Make sure the inside of the belt is clean.

Check the tracking, make sure it is still at "12:30."

Hector is making sure the belts and drums are cleaned every Sunday. This really seems to be helping to reduce maintenance issues, Ken B has seen a big improvement.

Hector suggested a training session for the line operators, learn about the tracking system and training with hands-on practice.

Another class on the valves related to cooling. Ken suggested a possible long term solution would be a pressure relief valve.

Develop visuals that could reinforce and remind what has been learned.

Line #2, need to put on a new drum, the line will be down two to three weeks. How will we manage this down time? It seems to be working OK for now. I think we could weld in the same gussets that we did on the other side and keep it going. We do have a spare in Orange but I would rather not use it unless we really need to.

There should be a step on the cleaning sheet to wash down the belt with cleaner, some operators just spray down the belt with water, but this does not remove everything.

Wrap up

Send all notes to Kimberly, put in a spreadsheet, group common items.

More complex idea might need a team to address them.

Note from Mary Watson—We received thirty-six leads for glitter at the IFT (Institute of Food Technologists) tradeshow. There were a total of 249 leads, about fifteen percent of the leads from the show were related to glitter.

Additional Shift

Idea put forward of moving to a four shift system. There would be two ten hour shifts Monday through Thursday with optional overtime to cover the four hours per day. There would also be two twelve hour shifts on Friday, Saturday, and Sunday. Thirty-six hour weekend shifts would be paid for forty hours to entice people to work it. Weekend people could also work overtime during the weekday shift, covering the four hour gap.

1. People seemed to like the idea of having three or four days off at a time if optional OT was available.
2. Second four shift system proposed: four six hour shifts work Monday through Wednesday. Then two shifts would work twelve hours on Thursday and Friday, and the two shifts would do twelve hours on

Saturday and Sunday. The twelve hour shift days would rotate so that everyone would still get a Saturday and Sunday off every other week.

This topic was combined and discussed in several different groups, below are combined suggestions/comments

Slitting Improvements

- Two people per slitter, utilize a "floater"
- Combined efforts and better training
- Quality over Quantity
- Exact packaging instructions, packing diagrams on slitting instructions, details of supplies, and weight measurements
- Standardize tare weights for packing materials
- Big waste of time if slitter is unaware that the master rolls contain breaks and bad areas because they have to stop and rewind and fix
- Color-coded flags for breaks, tears, holes, etc. for Master Rolls, to be used by line operators
- 320 mm cores are exactly 320 mm. Need to make them slightly wider to allow for "film drift" during slitting
- 320 mm, four inch, five inch spacers, etc.
- All slitting supplies available in the film warehouse i.e boxes, pallets, cores
- Possible to buy more knives and bars
- More storage space in slitting rooms

- Automatic set-up kits (set-up already measured), in designated bins with a diagram of each set up on the outside
- Additional slitter machine

Scheduling

- Optimize batch sizes for bigger batches
- Adjust reorder points for RM inventory
- More customer knowledge shared in the scheduling meeting
- Customer Service and Scheduler for film division
- Working relationships with the customers
- Can schedule immediately when orders received
- Better knowledge of film products = more accurate schedule
- Picker and Kitter in Orange to specialize and prioritize film kits
- Same for WH material handler
- Train a few people per shift to operate fork trucks
- Will film now be responsible for inventory management of kits, raws, and finished goods?
- Quality in off-shifts and weekends
- No one to approve color or particle size if batches start after 3:30 PM or on weekends
- Laminate glitter cards for color & shape
- Supervisors don't want responsibility of approving product

- Product Y—particle size passed test, but overall shape of glitter tended to be long pieces and several boxes were rejected by QC following batches made over the weekend. Resample and segregate took time
- Paperwork really needs to be reviewed by supervisors before coming upstairs. QC should not have to chase down people for signatures
- Film/Glitter samples should come up as quickly as possible so we can send for micro
- Shelf/box/rack to hold samples right next to stairwell door, so that anyone can bring samples up if they are coming upstairs anyway?
- Second QC/QA person working a swing shift to cover second and third shifts to help check paperwork and samples prior to first shift. AKA a Maria for Film

Communication

- Better communication between supervisors, shifts, and operators
- Better communication with instructions, take time to listen to what the operator is saying
- Dry erase board in room or Post it for visual communication
- Book for operators to record problems and solutions (problem and answer book)

- Log books only document production/product issues, need details of possible defects or problems
- Categorize log book ex: glitter, roll
- Cross training
- Upstairs vs. Downstairs—need open communication
- Create a line operator master roll form (checklist)

Other Topics

QC and Maintenance coverage on weekends/off shifts

Product Y—add half the amount of water at the beginning of batch

Forklift designated for the film department

Use a different windup for Z and X on line two

Yeah, seriously, can you believe it? All these great ideas from people who operate the equipment. All in just one day. Everyone was exhausted but psyched by what we had accomplished. These same people proceeded to implement all of these suggestions over the next few weeks. All on their own volition.

Appendix 2

ADDITIONAL RESOURCES

The Scientific Basis for Conscious Capitalism, Episode #57:

Conscious Capitalism: Here is a video of Raj Sisodia explaining Conscious Capitalism:

Teal Organizations: Teal Organizations are a type of company described by Fredric Laloux in his book titled, *Reinventing Organizations.* Guillaume Wiatr summarized Teal Organizations as:

A Teal organization is defined by the three following ideas in contrast to the paradigms of Amber, Orange and Green organizations:

1. *self-management* suggests a system based on peer relationships with no need for hierarchy, consensus, nor central command and control;
2. *wholeness* is about enabling employees to present their full personas rather than just their work personas;
3. *evolutionary purpose* is the idea to follow the natural evolution of how the organization grows

The paradigm is that an organization is similar to an organism in that the inner biology of the organism operates autonomously to sustain its health. This includes adapting to change, enabling employees to bring all their skills to the organization, and to do so without direct leadership.

A number of notable organizations around the world have adopted and operate with the Teal organization model some of which are in the table below.

Organization	Business, mission, or activity	Office location(s)	Refs.
Morning Star Co.	food processing	United States	[11]
Patagonia	apparel	United States	
Sounds True	media	United States	
AES	energy sector	international	
Buurtzorg	health care	Netherlands	

(Continued)

Organization	Business, mission, or activity	Office location(s)	Refs.
ESBZ	K-12 school	Germany	
Heiligenfeld	mental health hospitals	Germany	
Nucor	steel manufacturing	international	
Varkey Foundation	non-profit with expertise in Education	international	
Thomsen Trampedach	brand protection	Denmark	[12]

This short video does a very good job of explaining the main ideas in Laloux's book, *Reinventing Organizations.*

Interestingly, here is an overlap. Fredric Laloux speaking at a Conscious Capitalism leadership group:

https://www.bravenwork.com/ *Brave New Work* (Dignan 2019) is an excellent book and the accompanying website offers engaging topic-specific podcasts.

As I said in my introduction, I think Teal organizations are really a return to how human societies evolved to function over the last two hundred thousand years. This is what the research in the field of evolutionary psychology shows. It is also strongly supported by research in positive psychology. Evolutionary psychologists studying tribal groups have found that people behave altruistically and that leadership is fluid, depending on the needs of the group. It is not held by a "strong man." If I was going to give it a color, it would have to be infrared because it is our original and still the best human operating system. The "red" organization that Laloux (2014) posits as the first is actually a corruption of our natural state by a narcissistic sociopathic leader.

To further substantiate this argument, here are two quotes *Mismatch* by evolutionary psychologist Mark van Vugt and Ronald Giphart (2018):

"Amongst our ancestors the followers fundamentally created the leader." (p163.)

"In the savannah there were no managers or middle managers. Decisions were taken by the group, on the basis of consensus, not on the basis of hierarchy. Modern organizations have become excessively formalized and institutionalized, which goes against our small group instincts. Studies show that employees need a great deal of autonomy, a primeval preference for self-employment. People want to be left alone, they do not want some process supervisor breathing down their neck. The same studies reveal that employees consider autonomy and social contacts more important than pay. Our desires have not changed, only the circumstances in which we operate." (p145.)

This book has so much to offer, especially in the chapter on work, titled "This Isn't Working," and the chapter on leadership titled, "Follow the Leader."

In Conclusion

To recap all of the above, stick to the core principles and you can't go wrong. Maximize autonomy, intrinsically rewarding work and activities, cherish individuality and expression, minimal hierarchy/egalitarian, open information sharing (default to open), and purpose-related work. Remember, it's fractal; it works on a larger scale the same way it works on a small scale. What you are doing within your employee groups is what you should be doing with your suppliers, customers, community, and even competitors.

I would like to end with a final quote for you to keep in your back pocket, for times when you will surely need it:

"Self-interest is for the past, common-interest is for the future." David Attenborough in conversation with Greta Thunberg (BBC One).

I am eager to hear about your real-life examples of putting these principles into practice!

Learn More

The Connecticut Conscious Capitalism Chapter has developed a leadership course on Conscious Capitalism. For slide presentations and other materials, please email gwatson112455@gmail.com. For more information, please visit GavinWatsonAssociates.com.

Here you will find YouTube content, interviews, and podcasts with the Connecticut Chapter of Conscious Capitalism board members and others, including podcasts featuring Gavin Watson and David Sloan Wilson. Connecticut.ConsciousCapitalism.org

The Ready has created a series of truly excellent podcasts that are both fun and informative. The Ready constantly theorizes and experiments with radical work ideas in-house and with their clients. To listen to the podcast, visit BraveNewWork.com/Podcast.

Bibliography

INTRODUCTION

Atkins, Paul W.B., David Sloan Wilson, Steven C. Hayes. 2019. *Prosocial: Using Evolutionary Science to Build Productive, Equitable and Collaborative Groups.* Context Press.

Darwin, Charles. (1859) 2019. *On the Origin of Species.* S.L.: Alma Classics.

"Definition of BUSINESS." 2018. Merriam-Webster.com. 2018. https://www.merriam-webster.com/dictionary/business.

Feldman Barrett, Lisa. 2021. *Seven and a Half Lessons about the Brain.* S.L.: Picador.

Friedman, Milton. 1970. *A Friedman doctrine The Social Responsibility Of Business Is to Increase Its Profits.* The New York Times.

Haidt, Jonathan. 2006. *The Happiness Hypothesis : Putting Ancient Wisdom and Philosophy to the Test of Modern Science.* London: Arrow.

Laloux, Fredric. 2014. *Reinventing Organizations.* Nelson Parker.

Sisodia, Rajendra S., Jagdish N. Sheth, and David B. Wolfe. 2014. *Firms of Endearment : How World-Class Companies Profit from Passion and Purpose*. Upper Saddle River (N.J.): Pearson Education, Cop.

Wilson, David Sloan. 2016. *Does Altruism Exist? : Culture, Genes, and the Welfare of Others*. New Haven: Yale University Press.

Wilson, David Sloan, and Edward O. Wilson. 2007. "Rethinking the Theoretical Foundation of Sociobiology." *The Quarterly Review of Biology* 82 (4): 327–48. https://doi.org/10.1086/522809.

PART ONE

CHAPTER 1

Inc, Gallup. 2020. "Historic Drop in Employee Engagement Follows Record Rise." Gallup.com. July 2, 2020. https://www.gallup.com/workplace/313313/historic-drop-employee-engagement-follows-record-rise.aspx.

CHAPTER 2

Campbell, Joseph, Bill D. Moyers, and Betty S. Flowers. 2012. *The Power of Myth*. Turtleback Books.

Feldman Barrett, Lisa. 2021. *Seven and a Half Lessons about the Brain*. S.L.: Picador.

Rowling, J. K. 2007. *Harry Potter and the Deathly Hallows*. London: Bloomsbury.

The Muppets. 2020. "A Special Performance of 'Rainbow Connection' from Kermit the Frog, The Muppets." *YouTube*. https://www.youtube.com/watch?v=jS5fTzMP_mg.

Harari, Yuval Noah. (2011) 2019. *Sapiens: A Brief History of Humankind*. Random House UK.

CHAPTER 3

Dawkins, Richard. 1976. *The Selfish Gene*. Oxford: Oxford University Press.

Rand Ayn, Michael Dirda, Anna Balbusso, and Elena Balbusso. 2018. *Atlas Shrugged*. London: The Folio Society Ltd.

TED. 2015. "Margaret Heffernan: Why It's Time to Forget the Pecking Order at Work." *YouTube*. https://www.youtube.com/watch?v=Vyn_xLrtZaY.

Wheatley, Margaret J., and Myron Kellner-Rogers. 2003. *A Simpler Way*. San Francisco: Berrett-Koehler.

CHAPTER 4

Atkins, Paul W. B., David Sloan Wilson, and Steven C. Hayes. 2019. *Prosocial: Using Evolutionary Science to Build Productive, Equitable, and Collaborative Groups. Google Books*. New Harbinger Publications. https://books.google.com/books?hl=en&lr=&id=4RKaDwAAQBAJ&oi=fnd&pg=PT6&dq=prosocial+core+design+principles&ots=mcUIClMI3K&sig=y14bmRr2YtQE705910XNnOo5gRw#v=onepage&q=prosocial%20core%20design%20principles&f=false.

Darwin, Charles. (1859) 2019. *On the Origin of Species*. S.L.: Alma Classics.

"Extending Darwin's Revolution – David Sloan Wilson & Robert Sapolsky." n.d. www.youtube.com. Accessed June 7, 2022. https://www.youtube.com/watch?v=RsOIiW_Ec4c&t=629s.

Hare, Brian, Woods Vanessa. 2020. Survival of the Friendliest: *Understanding Our Origins and Rediscovering Our Common Humanity.* Oneworld Publications.

Wilson, David Sloan, and Edward O. Wilson. 2007. "Rethinking the Theoretical Foundation of Sociobiology." *The Quarterly Review of Biology* 82 (4): 327–48. https://doi.org/10.1086/522809.

Wilson, Sloan David. 2020. *This View of Life : Completing the Darwinian Revolution.* New York: Vintage Books, A Division Of Penguin Random House Llc.

CHAPTER 5

Lyubomirsky, Sonja. 2007. *The How of Happiness : A Practical Guide to Getting the Life You Want.* London Piatkus, Copyright.

Milne, A. A., and Walt Disney Enterprises. 1996. *Disney's Winnie the Pooh.* United States: Mouse Works.

Seligman, Martin E. P. 2011. *Flourish : A Visionary New Understanding of Happiness and Well-Being.* New York: Atria Paperback.

TED Blog Video. 2013. "Two Monkeys Were Paid Unequally: Excerpt from Frans de Waal's TED Talk." *YouTube.* https://www.youtube.com/watch?v=meiU6TxysCg.

Tutu, Desmond, The Dalai Lama, Douglas Abrams. 2016. *The Book of Joy : Lasting Happiness in a Changing World.* Diversified Publishing.

"You Aren't at the Mercy of Your Emotions – Your Brain Creates Them | Lisa Feldman Barrett." n.d. Www.youtube.com. Accessed June 7, 2022. https://www.youtube.com/watch?v=0gks6ceq4eQ&t=1s.

CHAPTER 6

"John Mackey: What's Love Got to Do with It?" n.d. www.
youtube.com. Accessed June 7, 2022. https://www.youtube.
com/watch?v=ED1R2zqdtCg.

Plomin, Robert. 2018. *Blueprint: How DNA Makes Us Who We Are*.
Mit Press.

CHAPTER 7

"A Conversation with Gary Hamel: Transformation of Leadership,
Step-By-Step." n.d. www.youtube.com. Accessed June 7, 2022.
https://www.youtube.com/watch?v=_mCmecrnLUM&t=1s.

Atkins, Paul W. B., David Sloan Wilson, and Steven C Hayes.
2019. *Prosocial : Using Evolutionary Science to Build Productive,
Equitable, and Collaborative Groups*. Oakland, Ca: Context
Press, An Imprint Of New Harbinger Publications.

Campbell, Joseph, Bill D. Moyers, and Betty S. Flowers. 2012. *The
Power of Myth*. Turtleback Books.

Carson, Clayborn, 2005. *The Papers of Martin Luther King, Jr.,
Volume V: Threshold of a New Decade, January 1959–December
1960*. University of California Press.

Christakis, Nicholas A. 2020. *Blueprint : The Evolutionary Origins
of a Good Society*. New York, Ny: Little, Brown Spark.

Feldman Barrett, Lisa. 2021. *Seven and a Half Lessons about the
Brain*. S.L.: Picador.

Gelbart, Larry. 1972. Review of *M*A*S*H*. CBS.

J R R Tolkien. 2014. *The Lord of the Rings*. London:
Harpercollinspublishers.

Jacobs, Lawrence, Alison Blank, Kristin Laskas Martin, and Jane
Startz. 1994. Review of *The Magic School Bus*. PBS.

Kegan, Robert, Lisa Laskow Lahey, Matthew L. Miller, Andy Fleming, and Deborah Helsing. 2016. *An Everyone Culture Becoming a Deliberately Developmental Organization.* Boston, Massachusetts Harvard Business Review Press.

Kohn, Alfie. 1999. *Punished by Rewards : The Trouble with Gold Stars, Incentive Plans, A's, Praise, and Other Bribes.* Boston ; New York: Mariner Books/Houghton Mifflin Harcourt.

Krames, Jeffrey A. 2016. *What the Best CEOs Know: 7 Exceptional Leadersand their Lessons for Transforming any Business.* McGraw Hill.

Mackey, John, and Raj Sisodia. 2014. *Conscious Capitalism : Liberating the Heroic Spirit of Business.* Boston, Mass.: Harvard Business Review Press.

Marquet, L. David. 2013. Turn the Ship Around: A True Story of Turning Followers into Leaders. New York: Portfolio.

___. 2018. "Leadership on a Submarine." Leadership Academy. (streaming video). https://www.youtube.com/watch?v=HYXH2XUfhfo&t=237s.

Mcchrystal, Stanley A. 2015. *Team of Teams : The Power of Small Groups in a Fragmented World.* London: Portfolio.

mlabvideo. 2013. "The Hierarchy of Human Capability." *YouTube.* https://www.youtube.com/watch?v=VlDxHfsW_-8.

"Podcast." n.d. Brave New Work. Accessed June 24, 2022. https://www.bravenewwork.com/podcast.

Shaw, Bernard. 2010. *Man and Superman : A Comedy and a Philosophy.* Los Angeles, Calif.: Indo-European Publishing.

"The Conscious Capitalists Podcast." n.d. ConsciousCapitalists. Accessed June 7, 2022. https://www.theconsciouscapitalists.com/.

Tutu, Desmond, The Dalai Lama, Douglas Abrams. 2016. *The Book of Joy : Lasting Happiness in a Changing World.* Diversified Publishing.

Tzu, Sun. 2019. *The Art of War*. Mineola, New York: Ixia Press.

United Nations. 2015. "Sustainable Development Goals."
United Nations Sustainable Development. United Nations.
2015. https://www.un.org/sustainabledevelopment/
sustainable-development-goals/.

Wheatley, Margaret. 2006. *Leadership and the New Science*.
Berrett-Koehler.

William Edwards Deming. 1986. *Out of the Crisis*. Cambridge,
Mass.: Massachusetts Institute Of Technology, Center For
Advanced Engineering Study.

William Edwards Deming. 2018. *The New Economics for Industry,
Government, Education*. Cambridge, Massachusetts Mit Press.

Wilson, David Sloan, and Edward O. Wilson. 2007.
"Rethinking the Theoretical Foundation of Sociobiology."
The Quarterly Review of Biology 82 (4): 327–48. https://doi.
org/10.1086/522809.

PART TWO

CHAPTER 8

"STOP STEALING DREAMS: Seth Godin at TEDxYouth@
BFS." n.d. www.youtube.com. Accessed June 7, 2022. https://
www.youtube.com/watch?v=sXpbONjV1Jc&t=1s.

CHAPTER 9

Mcgonigal, Jane. 2012. *Reality Is Broken : Why Games Make Us
Better and How They Can Change the World*. London: Vintage.

CHAPTER 16

"Industrial Electrical & Motor Repair Service CT | Traver IDC." n.d. www.traveridc.com. Accessed June 7, 2022. https://www. traveridc.com.

"Leanovations." n.d. www.leanovations.com. Accessed June 7, 2022. http://www.leanovations.com.

CHAPTER 18

Owen, Harrison. 2008. *Open Space Technology : A User's Guide.* San Francisco, Calif.: Berrett-Koehler Publishers.

Sinek, Simon. 2014. *Leaders Eat Last.* London, United Kingdom: Portfolio Penguin.

Vistage. 2014. "Leaders Eat Last | Simon Sinek." *YouTube.* https:// www.youtube.com/watch?v=4gUL76lV7gk.

"Wave Rider: Leadership for High Performance in a Self-Organizing World | OpenSpaceWorld.ORG." n.d. Openspaceworld.org. Accessed June 7, 2022. https:// openspaceworld.org/wp2/hho/wave-rider/.

APPENDICES

"BBC One – Greta Thunberg and Sir David Attenborough | Facebook | by BBC One | the Moving Moment Greta Thunberg and Sir David Attenborough Met in Person for the First Time." n.d. M.facebook.com. Accessed June 24, 2022. https://m.facebook.com/BBCOne/ videos/459761591975881/?locale2=sv_SE.

"Frederic Laloux, Author of 'Reinventing Organizations' | Modern Management | 2017 CEO Summit." n.d. Www.youtube.com.

Accessed June 7, 2022. https://www.youtube.com/
watch?v=2GlG_ESETgo&t=1s.

"Inno-Versity Presents: Raj Sisodia's Conscious Capitalism." n.d.
Www.youtube.com. Accessed June 7, 2022. https://www.
youtube.com/watch?v=DUEjfX4MV3g&t=1s.

Laloux, Frederic. 2014. *Reinventing Organizations : A Guide to
Creating Organizations Inspired by the next Stage of Human
Consciousness*. Brussels: Nelson Parker.

"Lean and Agile Adoption with the Laloux Culture Model,
Copyright Agile for All." n.d. Www.youtube.com.
Accessed June 7, 2022. https://www.youtube.com/
watch?v=g0Jc5aAJu9g&list=RDQMx6K2-LeCyQc&start_
radio=1.

Ronald Giphart, Mark Van Vugt, and Suzanne Heukensfeldt
Jansen. 2020. *Mismatch : How Our Stone Age Brain Deceives Us
Every Day (and What We Can Do about It)*. Editorial: London:
Robinson.

"Teal Organisation." 2022. Wikipedia. February 23, 2022.
https://en.wikipedia.org/wiki/
Teal_organisation#cite_note-huffpost1-6.

Wiatr, Guillaume. 2021. "Reinventing Organizations."
Metahelm. March 19, 2021. https://www.metahelm.com/
reinventing-organizations/

About the Author

Before joining his family's food manufacturing business, Gavin earned a BA in religious studies with a minor in psychology from Fairfield University. He then built a 30-foot wooden sailboat, which he lived on while starting a boat building and repair business. After joining Watson Inc. as a maintenance mechanic, he moved up through engineering and eventually became vice president of operations and company chair. Gavin focused on employee engagement through a self-organizing self-directed team approach. As a food manufacturer, Gavin has designed state-of-the-art edible film manufacturing equipment- and improved upon the designs of milling, blending, and fluid bed equipment.

Passionate about saving our planet's ecosystem at work and at home, he began purchasing 100% renewable electricity in 2010. He also mentored and encouraged teams running energy audits and implementing improvements that reduced electrical consumption by 25 percent while also growing the business at the same time.

In the 1990s, Gavin converted a Porsche 914 to an electric car and, later in the early 2000s, converted two diesel-powered cars to run on vegetable oil. For one of these, Gavin won most efficient biofuel vehicle and most environmentally friendly biofuel vehicle at the NESEA 2006 Tour de Sol.

He minimized hierarchy through self-organized, open space-style human operating systems in his organization. In 2019, his company sold for $89 million. Gavin is now chair of the Connecticut Chapter of Conscious Capitalism and is still a boat builder and a sailor. He just completed building a 19-foot double-ended yawl for cruising the Maine coast.

Connect with the author and get his most recent updates on his website:

GavinWatsonAssociates.com.

CPSIA information can be obtained
at www.ICGtesting.com
Printed in the USA
JSHW032254070223
37406JS00006B/9

9 781955 985796